MznLnx

Missing Links Exam Preps

Exam Prep for

Operations Management

Davis, Heineke, 5th Edition

The MznLnx Exam Prep is your link from the texbook and lecture to your exams.
The MznLnx Exam Preps are unauthorized and comprehensive reviews of your textbooks.

All material provided by MznLnx and Rico Publications (c) 2010
Textbook publishers and textbook authors do not particpate in or contribute to these reviews.

MznLnx

Rico Publications

Exam Prep for Operations Management
5th Edition
Davis, Heineke

Publisher: Raymond Houge
Assistant Editor: Michael Rouger
Text and Cover Designer: Lisa Buckner
Marketing Manager: Sara Swagger
Project Manager, Editorial Production: Jerry Emerson
Art Director: Vernon Lowerui

Product Manager: Dave Mason
Editorial Assitant: Rachel Guzmanji
Pedagogy: Debra Long
Cover Image: Jim Reed/Getty Images
Text and Cover Printer: City Printing, Inc.
Compositor: Media Mix, Inc.

(c) 2010 Rico Publications

ALL RIGHTS RESERVED. No part of this work covered by the copyright may be reproduced or used in any form or by an means--graphic, electronic, or mechanical, including photocopying, recording, taping, Web distribution, information storage, and retrieval systems, or in any other manner--without the written permission of the publisher.

For more information about our products, contact us at:
Dave.Mason@RicoPublications.com

For permission to use material from this text or product, submit a request online to:
Dave.Mason@RicoPublications.com

Printed in the United States
ISBN:

Contents

CHAPTER 1
Introduction to Operations Management — 1

CHAPTER 2
Operations Strategy: Defining How Firms Compete — 8

CHAPTER 3
The Role of Technology in Operations — 21

CHAPTER 4
Supply Chain Management — 32

CHAPTER 5
Integrating Manufacturing and Services — 41

CHAPTER 6
New Product and Service Development, and Process Selection — 45

CHAPTER 7
Project Management — 53

CHAPTER 8
Process Measurement and Analysis — 59

CHAPTER 9
Quality Management — 67

CHAPTER 10
Lean Production — 80

CHAPTER 11
Facility Location and Capacity — 86

CHAPTER 12
Facility Layouts — 93

CHAPTER 13
Aggregate Planning — 100

CHAPTER 14
Inventory Systems for Independent Demand — 107

CHAPTER 15
Inventory Systems for Dependent Demand — 112

CHAPTER 16
Waiting Line Management — 115

CHAPTER 17
Scheduling — 118

ANSWER KEY — 122

TO THE STUDENT

COMPREHENSIVE

The *MznLnx* Exam Prep series is designed to help you pass your exams. Editors at MznLnx review your textbooks and then prepare these practice exams to help you master the textbook material. Unlike study guides, workbooks, and practice tests provided by the texbook publisher and textbook authors, *MznLnx* gives you **all** of the material in each chapter in exam form, not just samples, so you can be sure to nail your exam.

MECHANICAL

The MznLnx Exam Prep series creates exams that will help you learn the subject matter as well as test you on your understanding. Each question is designed to help you master the concept. Just working through the exams, you gain an understanding of the subject--its a simple mechanical process that produces success.

INTEGRATED STUDY GUIDE AND REVIEW

MznLnx is not just a set of exams designed to test you, its also a comprehensive review of the subject content. Each exam question is also a review of the concept, making sure that you will get the answer correct without having to go to other sources of material. You learn as you go! Its the easiest way to pass an exam.

HUMOR

Studying can be tedious and dry. MznLnx's instructional design includes moderate humor within the exam questions on occassion, to break the tedium and revitalize the brain

Chapter 1. Introduction to Operations Management

1. _____ is the process of estimation in unknown situations. Prediction is a similar, but more general term. Both can refer to estimation of time series, cross-sectional or longitudinal data.
   a. 1990 Clean Air Act
   b. 28-hour day
   c. 33 Strategies of War
   d. Forecasting

2. An _____ is a subset of strategic work plan. It describes short-term ways of achieving milestones and explains how, or what portion of, a strategic plan will be put into operation during a given operational period, in the case of commercial application, a fiscal year or another given budgetary term. An operational plan is the basis for, and justification of an annual operating budget request.
   a. A Stake in the Outcome
   b. AAAI
   c. Operational planning
   d. A4e

3. _____ is an area of business concerned with the production of goods and services, and involves the responsibility of ensuring that business operations are efficient in terms of using as little resource as needed, and effective in terms of meeting customer requirements. It is concerned with managing the process that converts inputs (in the forms of materials, labour and energy) into outputs (in the form of goods and services.)

   Operations traditionally refers to the production of goods and services separately, although the distinction between these two main types of operations is increasingly difficult to make as manufacturers tend to merge product and service offerings.

   a. AAAI
   b. A4e
   c. A Stake in the Outcome
   d. Operations management

4. _____ is an organization's process of defining its strategy and making decisions on allocating its resources to pursue this strategy, including its capital and people. Various business analysis techniques can be used in _____, including SWOT analysis (Strengths, Weaknesses, Opportunities, and Threats) and PEST analysis (Political, Economic, Social, and Technological analysis) or STEER analysis involving Socio-cultural, Technological, Economic, Ecological, and Regulatory factors and EPISTEL (Environment, Political, Informatic, Social, Technological, Economic and Legal)

   _____ is the formal consideration of an organization's future course. All _____ deals with at least one of three key questions:

   1. 'What do we do?'
   2. 'For whom do we do it?'
   3. 'How do we excel?'

   In business _____, the third question is better phrased 'How can we beat or avoid competition?'. (Bradford and Duncan, page 1.)

   a. 28-hour day
   b. 33 Strategies of War
   c. Strategic planning
   d. 1990 Clean Air Act

Chapter 1. Introduction to Operations Management

5. _____ is one of the managerial functions like planning, organizing, staffing and directing. It is an important function because it helps to check the errors and to take the corrective action so that deviation from standards are minimized and stated goals of the organization are achieved in desired manner. According to modern concepts, _____ is a foreseeing action whereas earlier concept of _____ was used only when errors were detected. _____ in management means setting standards, measuring actual performance and taking corrective action.
   a. Schedule of reinforcement
   b. Turnover
   c. Decision tree pruning
   d. Control

6. _____ is an advertisement in which a particular product specifically mentions a competitor by name for the express purpose of showing why the competitor is inferior to the product naming it.

This should not be confused with parody advertisements, where a fictional product is being advertised for the purpose of poking fun at the particular advertisement, nor should it be confused with the use of a coined brand name for the purpose of comparing the product without actually naming an actual competitor. ('Wikipedia tastes better and is less filling than the Encyclopedia Galactica.')

In the 1980s, during what has been referred to as the cola wars, soft-drink manufacturer Pepsi ran a series of advertisements where people, caught on hidden camera, in a blind taste test, chose Pepsi over rival Coca-Cola.

   a. 33 Strategies of War
   b. 1990 Clean Air Act
   c. 28-hour day
   d. Comparative advertising

7. In organizational development (OD), _____ is the application of Socio-Technical Systems principles and techniques to the humanization of work.

The aims of _____ to improved job satisfaction, to improved through-put, to improved quality and to reduced employee problems, e.g., grievances, absenteeism.

Under scientific management people would be directed by reason and the problems of industrial unrest would be appropriately (i.e., scientifically) addressed.

   a. Graduate recruitment
   b. Management process
   c. Path-goal theory
   d. Work design

8. _____ refers to metrics and measures of output from production processes, per unit of input. Labor _____, for example, is typically measured as a ratio of output per labor-hour, an input. _____ may be conceived of as a metrics of the technical or engineering efficiency of production.
   a. Master production schedule
   b. Value engineering
   c. Remanufacturing
   d. Productivity

9. _____ is a business management strategy, initially implemented by Motorola, that today enjoys widespread application in many sectors of industry.

Chapter 1. Introduction to Operations Management 3

_____ seeks to improve the quality of process outputs by identifying and removing the causes of defects (errors) and variation in manufacturing and business processes. It uses a set of quality management methods, including statistical methods, and creates a special infrastructure of people within the organization ('Black Belts' etc.)

a. Takt time
b. Production line
c. Theory of constraints
d. Six sigma

10. _____ is the process of comparing the cost, cycle time, productivity, or quality of a specific process or method to another that is widely considered to be an industry standard or best practice. Essentially, _____ provides a snapshot of the performance of your business and helps you understand where you are in relation to a particular standard. The result is often a business case for making changes in order to make improvements.

a. Complementors
b. Cost leadership
c. Competitive heterogeneity
d. Benchmarking

11. _____ refers to training in different ways to improve overall performance. It takes advantage of the particular effectiveness of each training method, while at the same time attempting to neglect the shortcomings of that method by combining it with other methods that address its weaknesses.

Cross training is employee-employer field means, training employees to do one another's work.

a. 1990 Clean Air Act
b. 28-hour day
c. Cross-training
d. 33 Strategies of War

12. _____ is an inventory strategy that strives to improve the return on investment of a business by reducing in-process inventory and its associated carrying costs. To meet _____ objectives, the process relies on signals between different points in the process. This means the process is often driven by a series of signals, or Kanban , which tell production when to make the next part. Kanban are usually 'tickets' but can be simple visual signals, such as the presence or absence of a part on a shelf. Implemented correctly, _____ can dramatically improve a manufacturing organization's return on investment, quality, and efficiency.

a. 1990 Clean Air Act
b. 33 Strategies of War
c. 28-hour day
d. Just-in-time

13. _____ or lean production, which is often known simply as 'Lean', is a production practice that considers the expenditure of resources for any goal other than the creation of value for the end customer to be wasteful, and thus a target for elimination. Working from the perspective of the customer who consumes a product or service, 'value' is defined as any action or process that a customer would be willing to pay for. Basically, lean is centered around creating more value with less work.

a. Six Sigma
b. Theory of constraints
c. Lean manufacturing
d. Production line

14. _____, in microeconomics, are the cost advantages that a business obtains due to expansion. They are factors that cause a producer's average cost per unit to fall as scale is increased. _____ is a long run concept and refers to reductions in unit cost as the size of a facility, or scale, increases.

Chapter 1. Introduction to Operations Management

a. Economies of scope
b. Economies of scale
c. A4e
d. A Stake in the Outcome

15. A _____ is the system of organizations, people, technology, activities, information and resources involved in moving a product or service from supplier to customer. _____ activities transform natural resources, raw materials and components into a finished product that is delivered to the end customer. In sophisticated _____ systems, used products may re-enter the _____ at any point where residual value is recyclable.
  a. Drop shipping
  b. Packaging
  c. Supply chain
  d. Wholesalers

16. _____ is the management of a network of interconnected businesses involved in the ultimate provision of product and service packages required by end customers (Harland, 1996.) _____ spans all movement and storage of raw materials, work-in-process inventory, and finished goods from point of origin to point of consumption (supply chain.)

The definition an American professional association put forward is that _____ encompasses the planning and management of all activities involved in sourcing, procurement, conversion, and logistics management activities.

  a. Packaging
  b. Supply chain management
  c. Drop shipping
  d. Freight forwarder

17. A _____ is a computational model in the field of computer science that performs calculations using a biologically-inspired process. They are based upon the structure of biological cells, abstracting from the way in which chemicals interact and cross cell membranes. The concept was first introduced in a 1998 report by the computer scientist Gheorghe Paun, whose last name is the origin of the letter P in '_____s'.
  a. 28-hour day
  b. 1990 Clean Air Act
  c. 33 Strategies of War
  d. P system

18. _____ is the use of control systems (such as numerical control, programmable logic control, and other industrial control systems), in concert with other applications of information technology (such as computer-aided technologies [CAD, CAM, CAx]), to control industrial machinery and processes, reducing the need for human intervention. In the scope of industrialization, _____ is a step beyond mechanization. Whereas mechanization provided human operators with machinery to assist them with the physical requirements of work, _____ greatly reduces the need for human sensory and mental requirements as well.
  a. A Stake in the Outcome
  b. Automation
  c. AAAI
  d. A4e

19. _____ is a branch of operations research concerning itself with mathematical modeling and solution of problems concerning the placement of facilities in order to minimize transportation costs, avoid placing hazardous materials near housing, outperform competitors' facilities, etc.

A simple _____ problem is the Fermat-Weber problem, in which a single facility is to be placed, with the only optimization criterion being the minimization of the sum of distances from a given set of point sites. More complex problems considered in this discipline include the placement of multiple facilities, constraints on the locations of facilities, and more complex optimization criteria.

Chapter 1. Introduction to Operations Management 5

    a. Facility location   b. Multiscale decision making
    c. 1990 Clean Air Act   d. 28-hour day

20. _____ is, in very basic words, a position a firm occupies against its competitors.

According to Michael Porter, the three methods for creating a sustainable _____ are through:

1. Cost leadership

2. Differentiation

3. Focus (economics)

    a. 1990 Clean Air Act   b. Theory Z
    c. 28-hour day   d. Competitive advantage

21. _____ describes commerce transactions between businesses, such as between a manufacturer and a wholesaler, or between a wholesaler and a retailer. Contrasting terms are business-to-consumer (B2C) and business-to-government (B2G.)

The volume of B2B transactions is much higher than the volume of B2C transactions.

    a. Product bundling   b. Business-to-business
    c. Category management   d. Market environment

22. _____ is the provision of service to customers before, during and after a purchase.

According to Turban et al. (2002), '_____ is a series of activities designed to enhance the level of customer satisfaction - that is, the feeling that a product or service has met the customer expectation.'

Its importance varies by product, industry and customer; defective or broken merchandise can be exchanged, often only with a receipt and within a specified time frame.

    a. Service rate   b. 1990 Clean Air Act
    c. 28-hour day   d. Customer service

23. In economics, business, retail, and accounting, a _____ is the value of money that has been used up to produce something, and hence is not available for use anymore. In economics, a _____ is an alternative that is given up as a result of a decision. In business, the _____ may be one of acquisition, in which case the amount of money expended to acquire it is counted as _____.

    a. Cost allocation   b. Cost
    c. Cost overrun   d. Fixed costs

24. The _____ is a concept from business management that was first described and popularized by Michael Porter in his 1985 best-seller, Competitive Advantage: Creating and Sustaining Superior Performance.

A _____ is a chain of activities. Products pass through all activities of the chain in order and at each activity the product gains some value. The chain of activities gives the products more added value than the sum of added values of all activities. It is important not to mix the concept of the _____ with the costs occurring throughout the activities.

- a. Mass marketing
- b. Customer relationship management
- c. Market development
- d. Value chain

25. An _____ is a manufacturing process in which parts (usually interchangeable parts) are added to a product in a sequential manner using optimally planned logistics to create a finished product much faster than with handcrafting-type methods. The _____ developed by Ford Motor Company between 1908 and 1915 made _____s famous in the following decade through the social ramifications of mass production, such as the affordability of the Ford Model T and the introduction of high wages for Ford workers. However, the various preconditions for the development at Ford stretched far back into the 19th century, from the gradual realization of the dream of interchangeability, to the concept of reinventing workflow and job descriptions using analytical methods.

- a. A Stake in the Outcome
- b. A4e
- c. AAAI
- d. Assembly line

26. A _____ is a temporary alliance of enterprises that come together to share skills or core competencies and resources in order to better respond to business opportunities, and whose cooperation is supported by computer networks. It is a manifestation of Collaborative Networks and Distributed Collaborative Working.

There is much discussion regarding the definition of _____s.

- a. 28-hour day
- b. Virtual enterprise
- c. 1990 Clean Air Act
- d. Disintermediation

27. A _____ or business method is a collection of related, structured activities or tasks that produce a specific service or product (serve a particular goal) for a particular customer or customers. It often can be visualized with a flowchart as a sequence of activities.

There are three types of _____es:

1. Management processes, the processes that govern the operation of a system. Typical management processes include 'Corporate Governance' and 'Strategic Management'.
2. Operational processes, processes that constitute the core business and create the primary value stream. Typical operational processes are Purchasing, Manufacturing, Marketing, and Sales.
3. Supporting processes, which support the core processes. Examples include Accounting, Recruitment, Technical support.

A _____ begins with a customer's need and ends with a customer's need fulfillment. Process oriented organizations break down the barriers of structural departments and try to avoid functional silos.

Chapter 1. Introduction to Operations Management　　　7

　　a. 33 Strategies of War　　　　　　　　　b. 28-hour day
　　c. Business process　　　　　　　　　　d. 1990 Clean Air Act

28. _____ is subcontracting a process, such as product design or manufacturing, to a third-party company. The decision to outsource is often made in the interest of lowering cost or making better use of time and energy costs, redirecting or conserving energy directed at the competencies of a particular business, or to make more efficient use of land, labor, capital, (information) technology and resources. _____ became part of the business lexicon during the 1980s.
　　a. Unemployment insurance　　　　　　b. Outsourcing
　　c. Opinion leadership　　　　　　　　　d. Operant conditioning

29. A _____ is a type of bar chart that illustrates a project schedule. _____s illustrate the start and finish dates of the terminal elements and summary elements of a project. Terminal elements and summary elements comprise the work breakdown structure of the project.
　　a. Gantt chart　　　　　　　　　　　　b. 1990 Clean Air Act
　　c. 33 Strategies of War　　　　　　　　　d. 28-hour day

30. _____ is a theory of management that analyzes and synthesizes workflows, with the objective of improving labour productivity. The core ideas of the theory were developed by Frederick Winslow Taylor in the 1880s and 1890s, and were first published in his monographs, Shop Management and The Principles of _____ Taylor believed that decisions based upon tradition and rules of thumb should be replaced by precise procedures developed after careful study of an individual at work.
　　a. Master production schedule　　　　　b. Capacity planning
　　c. Value engineering　　　　　　　　　d. Scientific management

31. _____ in the USA, Canada, South Africa and Australia, and operational research in Europe, is an interdisciplinary branch of applied mathematics and formal science that uses methods such as mathematical modeling, statistics, and algorithms to arrive at optimal or near optimal solutions to complex problems. It is typically concerned with optimizing the maxima (profit, assembly line performance, crop yield, bandwidth, etc) or minima (loss, risk, etc.) of some objective function.
　　a. AAAI　　　　　　　　　　　　　　b. A Stake in the Outcome
　　c. A4e　　　　　　　　　　　　　　　d. Operations research

32. _____, is the discipline of using scientific research-based principles, strategies, and other analytical methods, such as mathematical modeling to improve any organization's ability to enact rational, meaningful business management decisions.
　　a. Cross ownership　　　　　　　　　　b. Workflow
　　c. Trustee　　　　　　　　　　　　　　d. Management science

Chapter 2. Operations Strategy: Defining How Firms Compete

1. _____ is the use of control systems (such as numerical control, programmable logic control, and other industrial control systems), in concert with other applications of information technology (such as computer-aided technologies [CAD, CAM, CAx]), to control industrial machinery and processes, reducing the need for human intervention. In the scope of industrialization, _____ is a step beyond mechanization. Whereas mechanization provided human operators with machinery to assist them with the physical requirements of work, _____ greatly reduces the need for human sensory and mental requirements as well.

   a. A Stake in the Outcome
   b. AAAI
   c. A4e
   d. Automation

2. _____, a business term, is a measure of how products and services supplied by a company meet or surpass customer expectation. It is seen as a key performance indicator within business and is part of the four perspectives of a Balanced Scorecard.

   In a competitive marketplace where businesses compete for customers, _____ is seen as a key differentiator and increasingly has become a key element of business strategy.

   a. Critical Success Factor
   b. Horizontal integration
   c. Foreign ownership
   d. Customer satisfaction

3. _____, in strategic management and marketing is, according to Carlton O'Neal, the percentage or proportion of the total available market or market segment that is being serviced by a company. It can be expressed as a company's sales revenue (from that market) divided by the total sales revenue available in that market. It can also be expressed as a company's unit sales volume (in a market) divided by the total volume of units sold in that market.

   a. Business-to-business
   b. Green marketing
   c. Market share
   d. Marketing plan

4. _____ is the provision of service to customers before, during and after a purchase.

   According to Turban et al. (2002), '_____ is a series of activities designed to enhance the level of customer satisfaction - that is, the feeling that a product or service has met the customer expectation.'

   Its importance varies by product, industry and customer; defective or broken merchandise can be exchanged, often only with a receipt and within a specified time frame.

   a. 1990 Clean Air Act
   b. 28-hour day
   c. Service rate
   d. Customer service

5. _____ is an advertisement in which a particular product specifically mentions a competitor by name for the express purpose of showing why the competitor is inferior to the product naming it.

   This should not be confused with parody advertisements, where a fictional product is being advertised for the purpose of poking fun at the particular advertisement, nor should it be confused with the use of a coined brand name for the purpose of comparing the product without actually naming an actual competitor. ('Wikipedia tastes better and is less filling than the Encyclopedia Galactica.')

   In the 1980s, during what has been referred to as the cola wars, soft-drink manufacturer Pepsi ran a series of advertisements where people, caught on hidden camera, in a blind taste test, chose Pepsi over rival Coca-Cola.

Chapter 2. Operations Strategy: Defining How Firms Compete

a. 1990 Clean Air Act
b. 33 Strategies of War
c. 28-hour day
d. Comparative advertising

6. The term '_____' refers to the concept of collecting information and attempting to spot a pattern in the information. In some fields of study, the term '_____' has more formally-defined meanings.

In project management _____ is a mathematical technique that uses historical results to predict future outcome.

a. Stepwise regression
b. Least squares
c. Regression analysis
d. Trend analysis

7. _____ is a branch of operations research concerning itself with mathematical modeling and solution of problems concerning the placement of facilities in order to minimize transportation costs, avoid placing hazardous materials near housing, outperform competitors' facilities, etc.

A simple _____ problem is the Fermat-Weber problem, in which a single facility is to be placed, with the only optimization criterion being the minimization of the sum of distances from a given set of point sites. More complex problems considered in this discipline include the placement of multiple facilities, constraints on the locations of facilities, and more complex optimization criteria.

a. Multiscale decision making
b. 1990 Clean Air Act
c. 28-hour day
d. Facility location

8. The _____ is a trilateral trade bloc in North America created by the governments of the United States, Canada, and Mexico. The agreement creating the trade bloc came into force on January 1, 1994. It superseded the Canada-United States Free Trade Agreement between the U.S. and Canada.

a. Career portfolios
b. Trade union
c. Business war game
d. North American Free Trade Agreement

9. _____ is the process of comparing the cost, cycle time, productivity, or quality of a specific process or method to another that is widely considered to be an industry standard or best practice. Essentially, _____ provides a snapshot of the performance of your business and helps you understand where you are in relation to a particular standard. The result is often a business case for making changes in order to make improvements.

a. Complementors
b. Benchmarking
c. Cost leadership
d. Competitive heterogeneity

10. _____ is the branch of economics that studies the dynamics of exchange rates, foreign investment, and how these affect international trade. It also studies international projects, international investments and capital flows, and trade deficits. It includes the study of futures, options and currency swaps.

a. A Stake in the Outcome
b. A4e
c. AAAI
d. International finance

11. A _____ is a general term that describes any government policy or regulation that restricts international trade. The barriers can take many forms, including the following terms that include many restrictions in international trade within multiple countries that import and export any items of trade.

- Import duty
- Import licenses
- Export licenses
- Import quotas
- Tariffs
- Subsidies
- Non-tariff barriers to trade
- Voluntary Export Restraints
- Local Content Requirements
- Embargo

Most _____s work on the same principle: the imposition of some sort of cost on trade that raises the price of the traded products. If two or more nations repeatedly use _____s against each other, then a trade war results.

a. Trade creation
c. Customs brokerage
b. Most favoured nation
d. Trade barrier

12. In economics, business, retail, and accounting, a _____ is the value of money that has been used up to produce something, and hence is not available for use anymore. In economics, a _____ is an alternative that is given up as a result of a decision. In business, the _____ may be one of acquisition, in which case the amount of money expended to acquire it is counted as _____.

a. Cost allocation
c. Cost
b. Fixed costs
d. Cost overrun

13. The _____ is given by the United States National Institute of Standards and Technology. Through the actions of the National Productivity Advisory Committee chaired by Jack Grayson, it was established by the Malcolm Baldrige National Quality Improvement Act of 1987 - Public Law 100-107 and named for Malcolm Baldrige, who served as United States Secretary of Commerce during the Reagan administration from 1981 until his 1987 death in a rodeo accident. APQC, , organized the first White House Conference on Productivity, spearheading the creation and design of the _____ in 1987, and jointly administering the award for its first three years.

a. Business Network Transformation
c. Scenario planning
b. Time and attendance
d. Malcolm Baldrige National Quality Award

14. _____ is a costing model that identifies activities in an organization and assigns the cost of each activity resource to all products and services according to the actual consumption by each: it assigns more indirect costs (overhead) into direct costs.

In this way an organization can establish the true cost of its individual products and services for the purposes of identifying and eliminating those which are unprofitable and lowering the prices of those which are overpriced.

In a business organization, the ABC methodology assigns an organization's resource costs through activities to the products and services provided to its customers.

a. A4e
b. Indirect costs
c. A Stake in the Outcome
d. Activity-based costing

15. An _____ is a manufacturing process in which parts (usually interchangeable parts) are added to a product in a sequential manner using optimally planned logistics to create a finished product much faster than with handcrafting-type methods. The _____ developed by Ford Motor Company between 1908 and 1915 made _____s famous in the following decade through the social ramifications of mass production, such as the affordability of the Ford Model T and the introduction of high wages for Ford workers. However, the various preconditions for the development at Ford stretched far back into the 19th century, from the gradual realization of the dream of interchangeability, to the concept of reinventing workflow and job descriptions using analytical methods.

a. Assembly line
b. AAAI
c. A4e
d. A Stake in the Outcome

16. _____, in microeconomics, are the cost advantages that a business obtains due to expansion. They are factors that cause a producer's average cost per unit to fall as scale is increased. _____ is a long run concept and refers to reductions in unit cost as the size of a facility, or scale, increases.

a. A Stake in the Outcome
b. A4e
c. Economies of scope
d. Economies of scale

17. _____, in marketing, manufacturing, call centres and management, is the use of flexible computer-aided manufacturing systems to produce custom output. Those systems combine the low unit costs of mass production processes with the flexibility of individual customization.

'_____' is the new frontier in business competition for both manufacturing and service industries.

a. 28-hour day
b. 1990 Clean Air Act
c. 33 Strategies of War
d. Mass customization

18. _____ refers to the difference between the cost of materials purchased by a company plus the cost of the labor to assemble a product and the price at which the company sells the product. An example is the price of gasoline at the pump over the price of the oil in it. In national accounts used in macroeconomics, it refers to the contribution of the factors of production, i.e., land, labor, and capital goods, to raising the value of a product and corresponds to the incomes received by the owners of these factors.

a. Rehn-Meidner Model
b. Deregulation
c. Minimum wage
d. Value added

19. A _____ is popular as a telecommunications industry term for non-core services or, in short, all services beyond standard voice calls and fax transmissions but, it can be used in ANY service industry (eg. Web 2.0) for the services providers provide for no cost to promote their main service business. In telecommunication industry on a conceptual level, _____s add value to the standard service offering, spurring the subscriber to use their phone more and allowing the operator to drive up their ARPU.

Chapter 2. Operations Strategy: Defining How Firms Compete

a. 28-hour day
b. 1990 Clean Air Act
c. 33 Strategies of War
d. Value-added service

20. _____ is something that a firm can do well and that meets the following three conditions:

Competencies are things that companys execute well across several business units or product sectors.

Firms usually have few competencies, but these are usually less liable to change rapidly.

1. It provides consumer benefits
2. It is not easy for competitors to imitate
3. It can be leveraged widely to many products and markets.

A _____ can take various forms, including technical/subject matter know-how, a reliable process and/or close relationships with customers and suppliers (Mascarenhas et al. 1998.)

a. NAIRU
b. Learning-by-doing
c. Dominant Design
d. Core competency

21. _____ refers to the overarching strategy of the diversified firm. Such a _____ answers the questions of 'in which businesses should we be in?' and 'how does being in these business create synergy and/or add to the competitive advantage of the corporation as a whole?'

Business strategy refers to the aggregated strategies of single business firm or a strategic business unit (SBU) in a diversified corporation. According to Michael Porter, a firm must formulate a business strategy that incorporates either cost leadership, differentiation or focus in order to achieve a sustainable competitive advantage and long-term success in its chosen arenas or industries.

a. Strategic group
b. Strategic drift
c. Competitive heterogeneity
d. Corporate strategy

22. _____ is a business Advocate term for an element which is necessary for an organization or project to achieve its mission. They are the critical factors or activities required for ensuring the success of your business. The term was initially used in the world of data analysis, and business analysis.

a. Collaborative leadership
b. Customer satisfaction
c. Critical success factor
d. Business hours

23. _____ is understood as a business unit within the overall corporate identity which is distinguishable from other business because it serves a defined external market where management can conduct strategic planning in relation to products and markets. When companies become really large, they are best thought of as being composed of a number of businesses (or _____ s.)

In the broader domain of strategic management, the phrase '_____' came into use in the 1960s, largely as a result of General Electric's many units.

a. Switching cost
b. Strategic business unit
c. Strategic drift
d. Strategic group

24. In quality assessment, _____ is an inspection standard describing the maximum number of defects that could be considered acceptable during the random sampling of an inspection. The defects found during inspection are classified into three levels: critical, major and minor. Broadly, these levels are defined as follows:

- Critical defects are those that render the product unsafe or hazardous for the end user, or that contravene mandatory regulations.

- Major defects can result in the product's failure, reducing its marketability, usability, or saleability.

- Minor defects do not affect the product's marketability or usability, but represent workmanship defects that make the product fall short of defined quality standards.

Different companies maintain different interpretations of each defect type.

a. A Stake in the Outcome
b. AAAI
c. A4e
d. Acceptable quality level

25. _____ is, in very basic words, a position a firm occupies against its competitors.

According to Michael Porter, the three methods for creating a sustainable _____ are through:

1. Cost leadership

2. Differentiation

3. Focus (economics)

a. 28-hour day
b. 1990 Clean Air Act
c. Theory Z
d. Competitive advantage

26. _____ or lean production, which is often known simply as 'Lean', is a production practice that considers the expenditure of resources for any goal other than the creation of value for the end customer to be wasteful, and thus a target for elimination. Working from the perspective of the customer who consumes a product or service, 'value' is defined as any action or process that a customer would be willing to pay for. Basically, lean is centered around creating more value with less work.

a. Six Sigma
b. Production line
c. Theory of constraints
d. Lean manufacturing

27. An _____ is a mostly hierarchical concept of subordination of entities that collaborate and contribute to serve one common aim.

Organizations are a variant of clustered entities. The structure of an organization is usually set up in many a styles, dependent on their objectives and ambience.

Chapter 2. Operations Strategy: Defining How Firms Compete

a. Organizational development
c. Organizational structure
b. Open shop
d. Informal organization

28. _____ are a set of documents that describe an organization's policies for operation and the procedures necessary to fulfill the policies. They are often initiated because of some external requirement, such as environmental compliance or other governmental regulations, such as the American Sarbanes-Oxley Act requiring full openness in accounting practices. The easiest way to start writing _____ is to interview the users of the _____ and create a flow chart or task map or work flow of the process from start to finish.

a. Horizontal integration
c. Customer retention
b. Group booking
d. Policies and procedures

29. A _____ is a computer program typically used to provide some form of artificial intelligence, which consists primarily of a set of rules about behavior. These rules, termed productions, are a basic representation found useful in AI planning, expert systems and action selection. A _____ provides the mechanism necessary to execute productions in order to achieve some goal for the system.

a. Production System
c. 28-hour day
b. 33 Strategies of War
d. 1990 Clean Air Act

30. _____ is a business management strategy, initially implemented by Motorola, that today enjoys widespread application in many sectors of industry.

_____ seeks to improve the quality of process outputs by identifying and removing the causes of defects (errors) and variation in manufacturing and business processes. It uses a set of quality management methods, including statistical methods, and creates a special infrastructure of people within the organization ('Black Belts' etc.)

a. Takt time
c. Production line
b. Six sigma
d. Theory of constraints

31. A _____ or business method is a collection of related, structured activities or tasks that produce a specific service or product (serve a particular goal) for a particular customer or customers. It often can be visualized with a flowchart as a sequence of activities.

There are three types of _____es:

1. Management processes, the processes that govern the operation of a system. Typical management processes include 'Corporate Governance' and 'Strategic Management'.
2. Operational processes, processes that constitute the core business and create the primary value stream. Typical operational processes are Purchasing, Manufacturing, Marketing, and Sales.
3. Supporting processes, which support the core processes. Examples include Accounting, Recruitment, Technical support.

A _____ begins with a customer's need and ends with a customer's need fulfillment. Process oriented organizations break down the barriers of structural departments and try to avoid functional silos.

Chapter 2. Operations Strategy: Defining How Firms Compete

a. 33 Strategies of War
b. 1990 Clean Air Act
c. 28-hour day
d. Business process

32. _____ is, in computer science and management, an approach aiming at improvements by means of elevating efficiency and effectiveness of the business process that exist within and across organizations. The key to _____ is for organizations to look at their business processes from a 'clean slate' perspective and determine how they can best construct these processes to improve how they conduct business. _____ Cycle.

_____ is also known as _____, Business Process Redesign, Business Transformation, or Business Process Change Management.

a. Personal management interview
b. Horizontal integration
c. Product life cycle
d. Business process reengineering

33. A _____ system is a manufacturing system in which there is some amount of flexibility that allows the system to react in the case of changes, whether predicted or unpredicted. This flexibility is generally considered to fall into two categories, which both contain numerous subcategories.

The first category, machine flexibility, covers the system's ability to be changed to produce new product types, and ability to change the order of operations executed on a part. The second category is called routing flexibility, which consists of the ability to use multiple machines to perform the same operation on a part, as well as the system's ability to absorb large-scale changes, such as in volume, capacity, or capability.

a. Manufacturing resource planning
b. Jidoka
c. Homeworkers
d. Flexible manufacturing

34. _____ is an inventory strategy that strives to improve the return on investment of a business by reducing in-process inventory and its associated carrying costs. To meet _____ objectives, the process relies on signals between different points in the process. This means the process is often driven by a series of signals, or Kanban , which tell production when to make the next part. Kanban are usually 'tickets' but can be simple visual signals, such as the presence or absence of a part on a shelf. Implemented correctly, _____ can dramatically improve a manufacturing organization's return on investment, quality, and efficiency.

a. 28-hour day
b. Just-in-time
c. 1990 Clean Air Act
d. 33 Strategies of War

35. _____ is the largest book retailer in the United States, operating mainly through its Barnes ' Noble Booksellers chain of bookstores headquartered in lower Fifth Avenue in Manhattan.

The company operates the chain of small 'B.

a. 33 Strategies of War
b. Barnes ' Noble, Inc.
c. 1990 Clean Air Act
d. 28-hour day

36. The _____ is a concept from business management that was first described and popularized by Michael Porter in his 1985 best-seller, Competitive Advantage: Creating and Sustaining Superior Performance.

A _____ is a chain of activities. Products pass through all activities of the chain in order and at each activity the product gains some value. The chain of activities gives the products more added value than the sum of added values of all activities. It is important not to mix the concept of the _____ with the costs occurring throughout the activities.

a. Customer relationship management
b. Mass marketing
c. Value chain
d. Market development

37. _____ refers to an assessment of the viability, stability and profitability of a business, sub-business or project.

It is performed by professionals who prepare reports using ratios that make use of information taken from financial statements and other reports. These reports are usually presented to top management as one of their bases in making business decisions.

a. Financial analysis
b. 28-hour day
c. 1990 Clean Air Act
d. 33 Strategies of War

38. In economics and business decision-making, _____ are costs that cannot be recovered once they have been incurred. _____ are sometimes contrasted with variable costs, which are the costs that will change due to the proposed course of action, and prospective costs which are costs that will be incurred if an action is taken.

In traditional microeconomic theory, only variable costs are relevant to a decision.

a. Cognitive biases
b. Sunk costs
c. Pygmalion effect
d. Fundamental attribution error

39. In economics, _____ are business expenses that are not dependent on the activities of the business They tend to be time-related, such as salaries or rents being paid per month. This is in contrast to variable costs, which are volume-related (and are paid per quantity.)

In management accounting, _____ are defined as expenses that do not change in proportion to the activity of a business, within the relevant period or scale of production.

a. Cost allocation
b. Cost of quality
c. Transaction cost
d. Fixed costs

40. _____s are expenses that change in proportion to the activity of a business. In other words, _____ is the sum of marginal costs. It can also be considered normal costs.

a. Cost overrun
b. Fixed costs
c. Variable Cost
d. Cost accounting

41. _____ are costs incurred on the purchase of land, buildings, construction and equipment to be used in the production of goods or the rendering of services. In other words, the total cost needed to bring a project to a commercially operable status. However, _____ are not limited to the initial construction of a factory or other business.

Chapter 2. Operations Strategy: Defining How Firms Compete   17

a. Capital costs
b. Contingent employment
c. Reservation wage
d. Fixed asset turnover

42. The _____ is an expected return that the provider of capital plans to earn on their investment.

Capital (money) used for funding a business should earn returns for the capital providers who risk their capital. For an investment to be worthwhile, the expected return on capital must be greater than the _____.

a. Capital intensive
b. 1990 Clean Air Act
c. Cost of capital
d. Weighted average cost of capital

43. _____ or economic opportunity loss is the value of the next best alternative forgone as the result of making a decision. _____ analysis is an important part of a company's decision-making processes but is not treated as an actual cost in any financial statement. The next best thing that a person can engage in is referred to as the _____ of doing the best thing and ignoring the next best thing to be done.
a. A Stake in the Outcome
b. Opportunity cost
c. AAAI
d. A4e

44. _____ are direct outlays of cash which may or may not be later reimbursed.

In operating a vehicle, gasoline, parking fees and tolls are considered _____ for the trip. Insurance, oil changes, and interest are not, because the outlay of cash covers expenses accrued over a longer period of time.

a. A4e
b. Out-of-pocket expenses
c. Ownership equity
d. A Stake in the Outcome

45. In management accounting, _____ establishes budget and actual cost of operations, processes, departments or product and the analysis of variances, profitability or social use of funds. Managers use _____ to support decision-making to cut a company's costs and improve profitability. As a form of management accounting, _____ need not follow standards such as GAAP, because its primary use is for internal managers, rather than outside users, and what to compute is instead decided pragmatically.
a. Quality costs
b. Transaction cost
c. Cost accounting
d. Marginal cost

46. _____ is the process of understanding, anticipating and influencing consumer behavior in order to maximize revenue or profits from a fixed, perishable resource This process was first discovered by Dr. Matt H. Keller. The challenge is to sell the right resources to the right customer at the right time for the right price.
a. Gap analysis
b. Yield management
c. Business model design
d. Business networking

47. In business and accounting, _____s are everything of value that is owned by a person or company. Any property or object of value that one possesses, usually considered as applicable to the payment of one's debts is considered an _____. Simplistically stated, _____s are things of value that can be readily converted into cash.
a. AAAI
b. A4e
c. A Stake in the Outcome
d. Asset

18   *Chapter 2. Operations Strategy: Defining How Firms Compete*

48. _____ is a term used in accounting, economics and finance to spread the cost of an asset over the span of several years.

In simple words we can say that _____ is the reduction in the value of an asset due to usage, passage of time, wear and tear, technological outdating or obsolescence, depletion, inadequacy, rot, rust, decay or other such factors.

In accounting, _____ is a term used to describe any method of attributing the historical or purchase cost of an asset across its useful life, roughly corresponding to normal wear and tear.

a. Treasury stock
b. Matching principle
c. Depreciation
d. Net profit

49. _____ are defined as identifiable non-monetary assets that cannot be seen, touched or physically measured, which are created through time and/or effort and that are identifiable as a separate asset. There are two primary forms of intangibles - legal intangibles (such as trade secrets (e.g., customer lists), copyrights, patents, trademarks, and goodwill) and competitive intangibles (such as knowledge activities (know-how, knowledge), collaboration activities, leverage activities, and structural activities.) Legal intangibles are known under the generic term intellectual property and generate legal property rights defensible in a court of law.

a. Employee value proposition
b. Interlocking directorate
c. Induction programme
d. Intangible assets

50. _____ is the state of being which occurs when a person, object, or service is no longer wanted even though it may still be in good working order. _____ frequently occurs because a replacement has become available that is superior in one or more aspects. Videotapes making way for DVDs

Technical _____ may occur when a new product or technology supersedes the old, and it becomes preferred to utilize the new technology in place of the old.

a. A4e
b. A Stake in the Outcome
c. Obsolescence
d. AAAI

51. The metastability in flip-flops can be avoided by ensuring that the data and control inputs are held valid and constant for specified periods before and after the clock pulse, called the _____ and the hold time (t_h) respectively. These times are specified in the data sheet for the device, and are typically between a few nanoseconds and a few hundred picoseconds for modern devices.

Unfortunately, it is not always possible to meet the setup and hold criteria, because the flip-flop may be connected to a real-time signal that could change at any time, outside the control of the designer.

a. 1990 Clean Air Act
b. 33 Strategies of War
c. 28-hour day
d. Setup time

52. In economics and finance, _____ is the change in total cost that arises when the quantity produced changes by one unit. It is the cost of producing one more unit of a good. Mathematically, the _____ function is expressed as the first derivative of the total cost (TC) function with respect to quantity (Q.)

a. Variable cost
b. Cost overrun
c. Transaction cost
d. Marginal Cost

53. In finance, _____, is the ratio of money gained or lost on an investment relative to the amount of money invested. The amount of money gained or lost may be referred to as interest, profit/loss, gain/loss, or net income/loss. The money invested may be referred to as the asset, capital, principal, or the cost basis of the investment.
    a. Return on sales
    b. Financial ratio
    c. Return on Capital Employed
    d. Rate of Return

54. _____ is the value on a given date of a future payment or series of future payments, discounted to reflect the time value of money and other factors such as investment risk. _____ calculations are widely used in business and economics to provide a means to compare cash flows at different times on a meaningful 'like to like' basis.

If offered a choice between $100 today or $100 in one year, everyone will choose $100 today.

    a. Net present value
    b. Present value
    c. 1990 Clean Air Act
    d. Discounted cash flow

55. _____ refers to the movement of cash into or out of a business or financial product. It is usually measured during a specified, finite period of time. Measurement of _____ can be used

- to determine a project's rate of return or value. The time of _____s into and out of projects are used as inputs in financial models such as internal rate of return, and net present value.
- to determine problems with a business's liquidity. Being profitable does not necessarily mean being liquid. A company can fail because of a shortage of cash, even while profitable.
- as an alternate measure of a business's profits when it is believed that accrual accounting concepts do not represent economic realities. For example, a company may be notionally profitable but generating little operational cash (as may be the case for a company that barters its products rather than selling for cash.) In such a case, the company may be deriving additional operating cash by issuing shares evaluating default risk, re-investment requirements, etc.

_____ is a generic term used differently depending on the context. It may be defined by users for their own purposes.

    a. Gross profit
    b. Cash flow
    c. Sweat equity
    d. Gross profit margin

56. In finance, the _____ approach describes a method of valuing a project, company, or asset using the concepts of the time value of money. All future cash flows are estimated and discounted to give their present values. The discount rate used is generally the appropriate WACC, that reflects the risk of the cashflows.
    a. Present value
    b. 1990 Clean Air Act
    c. Discounted cash flow
    d. Net present value

57. _____ or net present worth (NPW) is defined as the total present value (PV) of a time series of cash flows. It is a standard method for using the time value of money to appraise long-term projects. Used for capital budgeting, and widely throughout economics, it measures the excess or shortfall of cash flows, in present value terms, once financing charges are met.

a. 1990 Clean Air Act
c. Present value
b. Discounted cash flow
d. Net present value

58. The _____ of an edge is $c_f(u, v) = c(u, v) - f(u, v)$. This defines a residual network denoted $G_f(V, E_f)$, giving the amount of available capacity. See that there can be an edge from u to v in the residual network, even though there is no edge from u to v in the original network.
   a. 33 Strategies of War
   c. 28-hour day
   b. 1990 Clean Air Act
   d. Residual capacity

59. _____ in business and economics refers to the period of time required for the return on an investment to 'repay' the sum of the original investment. For example, a $1000 investment which returned $500 per year would have a two year _____. It intuitively measures how long something takes to 'pay for itself.' Shorter _____s are obviously preferable to longer _____s (all else being equal.)
   a. Novated lease
   c. Payback period
   b. Net worth
   d. Market value

60. The _____ is a rate of return used in capital budgeting to measure and compare the profitability of investments. It is also called the discounted cash flow rate of return (DCFROR) or simply the rate of return (ROR.) In the context of savings and loans the IRR is also called the effective interest rate.
   a. AAAI
   c. A4e
   b. A Stake in the Outcome
   d. Internal rate of return

Chapter 3. The Role of Technology in Operations

1. A _____ is a subset of the overall internal controls of a business covering the application of people, documents, technologies, and procedures by management accountants to solving business problems such as costing a product, service or a business-wide strategy. _____s are distinct from regular information systems in that they are used to analyze other information systems applied in operational activities in the organization. Academically, the term is commonly used to refer to the group of information management methods tied to the automation or support of human decision making, e.g. Decision Support Systems, Expert systems, and Executive information systems.

   a. 28-hour day
   b. Strategic information system
   c. Management information system
   d. 1990 Clean Air Act

2. _____ is, in very basic words, a position a firm occupies against its competitors.

   According to Michael Porter, the three methods for creating a sustainable _____ are through:

   1. Cost leadership

   2. Differentiation

   3. Focus (economics)

   a. 1990 Clean Air Act
   b. Theory Z
   c. 28-hour day
   d. Competitive advantage

3. In finance, the _____ approach describes a method of valuing a project, company, or asset using the concepts of the time value of money. All future cash flows are estimated and discounted to give their present values. The discount rate used is generally the appropriate WACC, that reflects the risk of the cashflows.

   a. 1990 Clean Air Act
   b. Net present value
   c. Present value
   d. Discounted cash flow

4. _____ is the process of extracting hidden patterns from data. As more data is gathered, with the amount of data doubling every three years, _____ is becoming an increasingly important tool to transform this data into information. It is commonly used in a wide range of profiling practices, such as marketing, surveillance, fraud detection and scientific discovery.

   a. 28-hour day
   b. Decision tree learning
   c. Data mining
   d. 1990 Clean Air Act

5. _____ is an integrated communications-based process through which individuals and communities discover that existing and newly-identified needs and wants may be satisfied by the products and services of others.

   _____ is defined by the American _____ Association as the activity, set of institutions, and processes for creating, communicating, delivering, and exchanging offerings that have value for customers, clients, partners, and society at large. The term developed from the original meaning which referred literally to going to market, as in shopping, or going to a market to buy or sell goods or services.

   a. Market development
   b. Customer relationship management
   c. Disruptive technology
   d. Marketing

Chapter 3. The Role of Technology in Operations

6. _____ is the intelligence of machines and the branch of computer science which aims to create it. Major _____ textbooks define the field as 'the study and design of intelligent agents,' where an intelligent agent is a system that perceives its environment and takes actions which maximize its chances of success. John McCarthy, who coined the term in 1956, defines it as 'the science and engineering of making intelligent machines.'

The field was founded on the claim that a central property of human beings, intelligence--the sapience of Homo sapiens--can be so precisely described that it can be simulated by a machine.

   a. AAAI
   b. A4e
   c. A Stake in the Outcome
   d. Artificial Intelligence

7. _____ is the use of control systems (such as numerical control, programmable logic control, and other industrial control systems), in concert with other applications of information technology (such as computer-aided technologies [CAD, CAM, CAx]), to control industrial machinery and processes, reducing the need for human intervention. In the scope of industrialization, _____ is a step beyond mechanization. Whereas mechanization provided human operators with machinery to assist them with the physical requirements of work, _____ greatly reduces the need for human sensory and mental requirements as well.

   a. AAAI
   b. A4e
   c. A Stake in the Outcome
   d. Automation

8. _____, a business term, is a measure of how products and services supplied by a company meet or surpass customer expectation. It is seen as a key performance indicator within business and is part of the four perspectives of a Balanced Scorecard.

In a competitive marketplace where businesses compete for customers, _____ is seen as a key differentiator and increasingly has become a key element of business strategy.

   a. Horizontal integration
   b. Critical Success Factor
   c. Customer satisfaction
   d. Foreign ownership

9. _____ is an area of business concerned with the production of goods and services, and involves the responsibility of ensuring that business operations are efficient in terms of using as little resource as needed, and effective in terms of meeting customer requirements. It is concerned with managing the process that converts inputs (in the forms of materials, labour and energy) into outputs (in the form of goods and services.)

Operations traditionally refers to the production of goods and services separately, although the distinction between these two main types of operations is increasingly difficult to make as manufacturers tend to merge product and service offerings.

   a. AAAI
   b. Operations management
   c. A Stake in the Outcome
   d. A4e

Chapter 3. The Role of Technology in Operations

10. An _____ is a manufacturing process in which parts (usually interchangeable parts) are added to a product in a sequential manner using optimally planned logistics to create a finished product much faster than with handcrafting-type methods. The _____ developed by Ford Motor Company between 1908 and 1915 made _____s famous in the following decade through the social ramifications of mass production, such as the affordability of the Ford Model T and the introduction of high wages for Ford workers. However, the various preconditions for the development at Ford stretched far back into the 19th century, from the gradual realization of the dream of interchangeability, to the concept of reinventing workflow and job descriptions using analytical methods.
    a. A Stake in the Outcome
    b. Assembly line
    c. AAAI
    d. A4e

11. _____ or lean production, which is often known simply as 'Lean', is a production practice that considers the expenditure of resources for any goal other than the creation of value for the end customer to be wasteful, and thus a target for elimination. Working from the perspective of the customer who consumes a product or service, 'value' is defined as any action or process that a customer would be willing to pay for. Basically, lean is centered around creating more value with less work.
    a. Six Sigma
    b. Production line
    c. Theory of constraints
    d. Lean manufacturing

12. An _____ is officially defined by ISO as an automatically controlled, reprogrammable, multipurpose manipulator programmable in three or more axes. The field of robotics may be more practically defined as the study, design and use of robot systems for manufacturing (a top-level definition relying on the prior definition of robot.)

Typical applications of robots include welding, painting, assembly, pick and place, packaging and palletizing, product inspection, and testing, all accomplished with high endurance, speed, and precision.

    a. A Stake in the Outcome
    b. A4e
    c. AAAI
    d. Industrial Robot

13. The metastability in flip-flops can be avoided by ensuring that the data and control inputs are held valid and constant for specified periods before and after the clock pulse, called the _____ and the hold time (t_h) respectively. These times are specified in the data sheet for the device, and are typically between a few nanoseconds and a few hundred picoseconds for modern devices.

Unfortunately, it is not always possible to meet the setup and hold criteria, because the flip-flop may be connected to a real-time signal that could change at any time, outside the control of the designer.

    a. 33 Strategies of War
    b. 28-hour day
    c. Setup time
    d. 1990 Clean Air Act

14. _____ in engineering is a method of manufacturing in which the entire production process is controlled by computer. The traditional separated process methods are joined through a computer by CIM. This integration allows that the processes exchange information with each other and they are able to initiate actions.
    a. Computer-integrated manufacturing
    b. 33 Strategies of War
    c. 1990 Clean Air Act
    d. 28-hour day

15. _____ is a company-wide computer software system used to manage and coordinate all the resources, information, and functions of a business from shared data stores.

An _____ system has a service-oriented architecture with modular hardware and software units and 'services' that communicate on a local area network. The modular design allows a business to add or reconfigure modules (perhaps from different vendors) while preserving data integrity in one shared database that may be centralized or distributed.

a. AAAI
b. Enterprise resource planning
c. A Stake in the Outcome
d. A4e

16. A _____ system is a manufacturing system in which there is some amount of flexibility that allows the system to react in the case of changes, whether predicted or unpredicted. This flexibility is generally considered to fall into two categories, which both contain numerous subcategories.

The first category, machine flexibility, covers the system's ability to be changed to produce new product types, and ability to change the order of operations executed on a part. The second category is called routing flexibility, which consists of the ability to use multiple machines to perform the same operation on a part, as well as the system's ability to absorb large-scale changes, such as in volume, capacity, or capability.

a. Manufacturing resource planning
b. Homeworkers
c. Jidoka
d. Flexible manufacturing

17. _____ consists of the processes a company uses to track and organize its contacts with its current and prospective customers. _____ software is used to support these processes; information about customers and customer interactions can be entered, stored and accessed by employees in different company departments. Typical _____ goals are to improve services provided to customers, and to use customer contact information for targeted marketing.

a. Marketing plan
b. Disruptive technology
c. Customer relationship management
d. Green marketing

18. Manufacturing Resource Planning (_____) is defined by APICS as a method for the effective planning of all resources of a manufacturing company. Ideally, it addresses operational planning in units, financial planning in dollars, and has a simulation capability to answer 'what-if' questions and extension of closed-loop MRP. Manufacturing Resource Planning (or MRP2) - Around 1980, over-frequent changes in sales forecasts, entailing continual readjustments in production, as well as the unsuitability of the parameters fixed by the system, led MRP (Material Requirement Planning) to evolve into a new concept : Manufacturing Resource Planning (e.g. MRP 2)

This is not exclusively a software function, but a marriage of people skills, dedication to data base accuracy, and computer resources.

a. Homeworkers
b. Manufacturing resource planning
c. MRP II
d. Jidoka

Chapter 3. The Role of Technology in Operations

19. In business and engineering, _____ is the term used to describe the complete process of bringing a new product or service to market. There are two parallel paths involved in the _____ process: one involves the idea generation, product design, and detail engineering; the other involves market research and marketing analysis. Companies typically see _____ as the first stage in generating and commercializing new products within the overall strategic process of product life cycle management used to maintain or grow their market share.

   a. 28-hour day
   b. 1990 Clean Air Act
   c. New product development
   d. 33 Strategies of War

20. A _____ is the system of organizations, people, technology, activities, information and resources involved in moving a product or service from supplier to customer. _____ activities transform natural resources, raw materials and components into a finished product that is delivered to the end customer. In sophisticated _____ systems, used products may re-enter the _____ at any point where residual value is recyclable.

   a. Wholesalers
   b. Packaging
   c. Drop shipping
   d. Supply chain

21. _____ is the management of a network of interconnected businesses involved in the ultimate provision of product and service packages required by end customers (Harland, 1996.) _____ spans all movement and storage of raw materials, work-in-process inventory, and finished goods from point of origin to point of consumption (supply chain.)

The definition an American professional association put forward is that _____ encompasses the planning and management of all activities involved in sourcing, procurement, conversion, and logistics management activities.

   a. Freight forwarder
   b. Supply chain management
   c. Drop shipping
   d. Packaging

22. _____ is a business term which refers to a range of software tools or modules used in executing supply chain transactions, managing supplier relationships and controlling associated business processes.

While functionality in such systems can often be broad - it commonly includes:

   1. Customer requirement processing
   2. Purchase order processing
   3. Inventory management
   4. Goods receipt and Warehouse management
   5. Supplier Management/Sourcing

A requirement of many _____ often includes forecasting. Such tools often attempt to balance the disparity between supply and demand by improving business processes and using algorithms and consumption analysis to better plan future needs. _____ also often includes integration technology that allows organizations to trade electronically with supply chain partners.

   a. Supply-Chain Operations Reference
   b. Demand chain
   c. Supply chain management software
   d. Vendor Managed Inventory

Chapter 3. The Role of Technology in Operations

23. In business and engineering, new _____ is the term used to describe the complete process of bringing a new product or service to market. There are two parallel paths involved in the NProduct development process: one involves the idea generation, product design, and detail engineering; the other involves market research and marketing analysis. Companies typically see new _____ as the first stage in generating and commercializing new products within the overall strategic process of product life cycle management used to maintain or grow their market share.
   - a. 28-hour day
   - b. 1990 Clean Air Act
   - c. 33 Strategies of War
   - d. Product development

24. _____ is an advertisement in which a particular product specifically mentions a competitor by name for the express purpose of showing why the competitor is inferior to the product naming it.

This should not be confused with parody advertisements, where a fictional product is being advertised for the purpose of poking fun at the particular advertisement, nor should it be confused with the use of a coined brand name for the purpose of comparing the product without actually naming an actual competitor. ('Wikipedia tastes better and is less filling than the Encyclopedia Galactica.')

In the 1980s, during what has been referred to as the cola wars, soft-drink manufacturer Pepsi ran a series of advertisements where people, caught on hidden camera, in a blind taste test, chose Pepsi over rival Coca-Cola.

   - a. 33 Strategies of War
   - b. 1990 Clean Air Act
   - c. Comparative advertising
   - d. 28-hour day

25. _____ is a branch of operations research concerning itself with mathematical modeling and solution of problems concerning the placement of facilities in order to minimize transportation costs, avoid placing hazardous materials near housing, outperform competitors' facilities, etc.

A simple _____ problem is the Fermat-Weber problem, in which a single facility is to be placed, with the only optimization criterion being the minimization of the sum of distances from a given set of point sites. More complex problems considered in this discipline include the placement of multiple facilities, constraints on the locations of facilities, and more complex optimization criteria.

   - a. Facility location
   - b. Multiscale decision making
   - c. 28-hour day
   - d. 1990 Clean Air Act

26. _____ is subcontracting a process, such as product design or manufacturing, to a third-party company. The decision to outsource is often made in the interest of lowering cost or making better use of time and energy costs, redirecting or conserving energy directed at the competencies of a particular business, or to make more efficient use of land, labor, capital, (information) technology and resources. _____ became part of the business lexicon during the 1980s.
   - a. Operant conditioning
   - b. Opinion leadership
   - c. Outsourcing
   - d. Unemployment insurance

27. In economics, _____ is the removal of intermediaries in a supply chain: 'cutting out the middleman'. Instead of going through traditional distribution channels, which had some type of intermediate (such as a distributor, wholesaler, broker, or agent), companies may now deal with every customer directly, for example via the Internet. One important factor is a drop in the cost of servicing customers directly.

a. Virtual enterprise
c. 1990 Clean Air Act
b. 28-hour day
d. Disintermediation

28. _____ is the process of estimation in unknown situations. Prediction is a similar, but more general term. Both can refer to estimation of time series, cross-sectional or longitudinal data.

a. 1990 Clean Air Act
c. 28-hour day
b. 33 Strategies of War
d. Forecasting

29. _____ is an organization's process of defining its strategy and making decisions on allocating its resources to pursue this strategy, including its capital and people. Various business analysis techniques can be used in _____, including SWOT analysis (Strengths, Weaknesses, Opportunities, and Threats) and PEST analysis (Political, Economic, Social, and Technological analysis) or STEER analysis involving Socio-cultural, Technological, Economic, Ecological, and Regulatory factors and EPISTEL (Environment, Political, Informatic, Social, Technological, Economic and Legal)

_____ is the formal consideration of an organization's future course. All _____ deals with at least one of three key questions:

1. 'What do we do?'
2. 'For whom do we do it?'
3. 'How do we excel?'

In business _____, the third question is better phrased 'How can we beat or avoid competition?'. (Bradford and Duncan, page 1.)

a. 33 Strategies of War
c. Strategic planning
b. 1990 Clean Air Act
d. 28-hour day

30. A _____ is a process in which a potential employee is evaluated by an employer for prospective employment in their company, organization and was established in the late 16th century.

A _____ typically precedes the hiring decision, and is used to evaluate the candidate. The interview is usually preceded by the evaluation of submitted résumés from interested candidates, then selecting a small number of candidates for interviews.

a. Split shift
c. Job interview
b. Supported employment
d. Payrolling

31. _____ is the provision of service to customers before, during and after a purchase.

According to Turban et al. (2002), '_____ is a series of activities designed to enhance the level of customer satisfaction - that is, the feeling that a product or service has met the customer expectation.'

Its importance varies by product, industry and customer; defective or broken merchandise can be exchanged, often only with a receipt and within a specified time frame.

a. Service rate
b. Customer service
c. 28-hour day
d. 1990 Clean Air Act

32. _____, in marketing, manufacturing, call centres and management, is the use of flexible computer-aided manufacturing systems to produce custom output. Those systems combine the low unit costs of mass production processes with the flexibility of individual customization.

'_____' is the new frontier in business competition for both manufacturing and service industries.

a. 33 Strategies of War
b. Mass customization
c. 1990 Clean Air Act
d. 28-hour day

33. _____ consists of the sale of goods or merchandise from a fixed location, such as a department store, boutique or kiosk in small or individual lots for direct consumption by the purchaser. _____ may include subordinated services, such as delivery. Purchasers may be individuals or businesses.

a. 28-hour day
b. Retailing
c. Planogram
d. 1990 Clean Air Act

34. In economics, business, retail, and accounting, a _____ is the value of money that has been used up to produce something, and hence is not available for use anymore. In economics, a _____ is an alternative that is given up as a result of a decision. In business, the _____ may be one of acquisition, in which case the amount of money expended to acquire it is counted as _____.

a. Cost overrun
b. Fixed costs
c. Cost allocation
d. Cost

35. _____, in microeconomics, are the cost advantages that a business obtains due to expansion. They are factors that cause a producer's average cost per unit to fall as scale is increased. _____ is a long run concept and refers to reductions in unit cost as the size of a facility, or scale, increases.

a. Economies of scope
b. A Stake in the Outcome
c. A4e
d. Economies of scale

36. In organizational development (OD), _____ is the application of Socio-Technical Systems principles and techniques to the humanization of work.

The aims of _____ to improved job satisfaction, to improved through-put, to improved quality and to reduced employee problems, e.g., grievances, absenteeism.

Under scientific management people would be directed by reason and the problems of industrial unrest would be appropriately (i.e., scientifically) addressed.

a. Management process
b. Path-goal theory
c. Graduate recruitment
d. Work design

37. _____ is a costing model that identifies activities in an organization and assigns the cost of each activity resource to all products and services according to the actual consumption by each: it assigns more indirect costs (overhead) into direct costs.

Chapter 3. The Role of Technology in Operations

In this way an organization can establish the true cost of its individual products and services for the purposes of identifying and eliminating those which are unprofitable and lowering the prices of those which are overpriced.

In a business organization, the ABC methodology assigns an organization's resource costs through activities to the products and services provided to its customers.

a. Indirect costs
b. A4e
c. A Stake in the Outcome
d. Activity-based costing

38. _____ refers to training in different ways to improve overall performance. It takes advantage of the particular effectiveness of each training method, while at the same time attempting to neglect the shortcomings of that method by combining it with other methods that address its weaknesses.

Cross training is employee-employer field means, training employees to do one another's work.

a. 33 Strategies of War
b. 1990 Clean Air Act
c. 28-hour day
d. Cross-training

39. An _____ is a private computer network that uses Internet technologies to securely share any part of an organization's information or operational systems with its employees. Sometimes the term refers only to the organization's internal website, but often it is a more extensive part of the organization's computer infrastructure and private websites are an important component and focal point of internal communication and collaboration.

An _____ is built from the same concepts and technologies used for the Internet, such as client-server computing and the Internet Protocol Suite (TCP/IP.)

a. A4e
b. AAAI
c. Intranet
d. A Stake in the Outcome

40. A _____ or business method is a collection of related, structured activities or tasks that produce a specific service or product (serve a particular goal) for a particular customer or customers. It often can be visualized with a flowchart as a sequence of activities.

There are three types of _____ es:

1. Management processes, the processes that govern the operation of a system. Typical management processes include 'Corporate Governance' and 'Strategic Management'.
2. Operational processes, processes that constitute the core business and create the primary value stream. Typical operational processes are Purchasing, Manufacturing, Marketing, and Sales.
3. Supporting processes, which support the core processes. Examples include Accounting, Recruitment, Technical support.

A _____ begins with a customer's need and ends with a customer's need fulfillment. Process oriented organizations break down the barriers of structural departments and try to avoid functional silos.

Chapter 3. The Role of Technology in Operations

a. 28-hour day
b. 1990 Clean Air Act
c. 33 Strategies of War
d. Business process

41. _____ is the largest book retailer in the United States, operating mainly through its Barnes ' Noble Booksellers chain of bookstores headquartered in lower Fifth Avenue in Manhattan.

The company operates the chain of small 'B.

a. Barnes ' Noble, Inc.
b. 1990 Clean Air Act
c. 33 Strategies of War
d. 28-hour day

42. _____ describes commerce transactions between businesses, such as between a manufacturer and a wholesaler, or between a wholesaler and a retailer. Contrasting terms are business-to-consumer (B2C) and business-to-government (B2G.)

The volume of B2B transactions is much higher than the volume of B2C transactions.

a. Market environment
b. Category management
c. Product bundling
d. Business-to-business

43. An _____ is a private network that uses Internet protocols, network connectivity, and possibly the public telecommunication system to securely share part of an organization's information or operations with suppliers, vendors, partners, customers or other businesses. An _____ can be viewed as part of a company's intranet that is extended to users outside the company (e.g.: normally over the Internet.) It has also been described as a 'state of mind' in which the Internet is perceived as a way to do business with a preapproved set of other companies business-to-business (B2B), in isolation from all other Internet users.

a. A4e
b. A Stake in the Outcome
c. AAAI
d. Extranet

44. Procter is a surname, and may also refer to:

- Bryan Waller Procter (pseud. Barry Cornwall), English poet
- Goodwin Procter, American law firm
- _____, consumer products multinational

a. Downstream
b. Master and Servant Acts
c. Strict liability
d. Procter ' Gamble

45. _____ refers to the difference between the cost of materials purchased by a company plus the cost of the labor to assemble a product and the price at which the company sells the product. An example is the price of gasoline at the pump over the price of the oil in it. In national accounts used in macroeconomics, it refers to the contribution of the factors of production, i.e., land, labor, and capital goods, to raising the value of a product and corresponds to the incomes received by the owners of these factors.

a. Rehn-Meidner Model   b. Minimum wage
c. Deregulation   d. Value added

46. _____ refers to the structured transmission of data between organizations by electronic means. It is used to transfer electronic documents from one computer system to another (ie) from one trading partner to another trading partner. It is more than mere E-mail; for instance, organizations might replace bills of lading and even checks with appropriate _____ messages.

a. Electronic data interchange   b. A Stake in the Outcome
c. AAAI   d. A4e

47. In economics and especially in the theory of competition, _____ are obstacles in the path of a firm that make it difficult to enter a given market.

_____ are the source of a firm's pricing power - the ability of a firm to raise prices without losing all its customers.

The term refers to hindrances that an individual may face while trying to gain entrance into a profession or trade.

a. 1990 Clean Air Act   b. Predatory pricing
c. 28-hour day   d. Barriers to entry

Chapter 4. Supply Chain Management

1. In economics, _____s are key economic variables that economists used to predict a new phase of the business cycle. A _____ is one that changes before the economy does; a lagging indicator is one that changes after the economy has changed. Examples of _____s include stock prices, which often improve or worsen before a similar change in the economy.

   a. Perfect competition
   b. Deflation
   c. Human capital
   d. Leading indicator

2. _____ is a business management strategy, initially implemented by Motorola, that today enjoys widespread application in many sectors of industry.

   _____ seeks to improve the quality of process outputs by identifying and removing the causes of defects (errors) and variation in manufacturing and business processes. It uses a set of quality management methods, including statistical methods, and creates a special infrastructure of people within the organization ('Black Belts' etc.)

   a. Takt time
   b. Production line
   c. Theory of constraints
   d. Six sigma

3. _____ is an advertisement in which a particular product specifically mentions a competitor by name for the express purpose of showing why the competitor is inferior to the product naming it.

   This should not be confused with parody advertisements, where a fictional product is being advertised for the purpose of poking fun at the particular advertisement, nor should it be confused with the use of a coined brand name for the purpose of comparing the product without actually naming an actual competitor. ('Wikipedia tastes better and is less filling than the Encyclopedia Galactica.')

   In the 1980s, during what has been referred to as the cola wars, soft-drink manufacturer Pepsi ran a series of advertisements where people, caught on hidden camera, in a blind taste test, chose Pepsi over rival Coca-Cola.

   a. 1990 Clean Air Act
   b. 33 Strategies of War
   c. 28-hour day
   d. Comparative advertising

4. _____ is the management of the flow of goods, information and other resources, including energy and people, between the point of origin and the point of consumption in order to meet the requirements of consumers (frequently, and originally, military organizations.) _____ involves the integration of information, transportation, inventory, warehousing, material-handling, and packaging, and occasionally security. _____ is a channel of the supply chain which adds the value of time and place utility.

   a. Third-party logistics
   b. 1990 Clean Air Act
   c. 28-hour day
   d. Logistics

5. A _____ is the system of organizations, people, technology, activities, information and resources involved in moving a product or service from supplier to customer. _____ activities transform natural resources, raw materials and components into a finished product that is delivered to the end customer. In sophisticated _____ systems, used products may re-enter the _____ at any point where residual value is recyclable.

   a. Wholesalers
   b. Packaging
   c. Drop shipping
   d. Supply chain

Chapter 4. Supply Chain Management

6. _____ is the management of a network of interconnected businesses involved in the ultimate provision of product and service packages required by end customers (Harland, 1996.) _____ spans all movement and storage of raw materials, work-in-process inventory, and finished goods from point of origin to point of consumption (supply chain.)

The definition an American professional association put forward is that _____ encompasses the planning and management of all activities involved in sourcing, procurement, conversion, and logistics management activities.

- a. Freight forwarder
- b. Packaging
- c. Drop shipping
- d. Supply chain management

7. _____ is the process of estimation in unknown situations. Prediction is a similar, but more general term. Both can refer to estimation of time series, cross-sectional or longitudinal data.
- a. 33 Strategies of War
- b. 28-hour day
- c. 1990 Clean Air Act
- d. Forecasting

8. _____ is an inventory strategy that strives to improve the return on investment of a business by reducing in-process inventory and its associated carrying costs. To meet _____ objectives, the process relies on signals between different points in the process. This means the process is often driven by a series of signals, or Kanban , which tell production when to make the next part. Kanban are usually 'tickets' but can be simple visual signals, such as the presence or absence of a part on a shelf. Implemented correctly, _____ can dramatically improve a manufacturing organization's return on investment, quality, and efficiency.
- a. 28-hour day
- b. 1990 Clean Air Act
- c. 33 Strategies of War
- d. Just-in-time

9. _____ is a concept related to lean and just-in-time (JIT) production. The Japanese word _____ is a common term meaning 'signboard' or 'billboard'. According to Taiichi Ohno, the man credited with developing JIT, _____ is a means through which JIT is achieved.
- a. Kanban
- b. Succession planning
- c. Risk management
- d. Trademark

10. In microeconomics and management, the term _____ describes a style of management control. Vertically integrated companies are united through a hierarchy with a common owner. Usually each member of the hierarchy produces a different product or (market-specific) service, and the products combine to satisfy a common need.
- a. 33 Strategies of War
- b. Vertical integration
- c. 28-hour day
- d. 1990 Clean Air Act

11. _____ or lean production, which is often known simply as 'Lean', is a production practice that considers the expenditure of resources for any goal other than the creation of value for the end customer to be wasteful, and thus a target for elimination. Working from the perspective of the customer who consumes a product or service, 'value' is defined as any action or process that a customer would be willing to pay for. Basically, lean is centered around creating more value with less work.
- a. Production line
- b. Six Sigma
- c. Theory of constraints
- d. Lean manufacturing

Chapter 4. Supply Chain Management

12. The _____ Automobile Company is an automobile manufacturer based in Wolfsburg, Germany, and is the original brand within the _____ Group, as well as the largest brand by sales volume.

_____ means 'people's car' in German, in which it is pronounced . Its current tagline or slogan is Das Auto .

 a. Volkswagen
 b. Turnover
 c. Competence-based Strategic Management
 d. Rate of return

13. An _____ is a manufacturing process in which parts (usually interchangeable parts) are added to a product in a sequential manner using optimally planned logistics to create a finished product much faster than with handcrafting-type methods. The _____ developed by Ford Motor Company between 1908 and 1915 made _____s famous in the following decade through the social ramifications of mass production, such as the affordability of the Ford Model T and the introduction of high wages for Ford workers. However, the various preconditions for the development at Ford stretched far back into the 19th century, from the gradual realization of the dream of interchangeability, to the concept of reinventing workflow and job descriptions using analytical methods.

 a. A Stake in the Outcome
 b. Assembly line
 c. AAAI
 d. A4e

14. The _____ is an observed phenomenon in forecast-driven distribution channels. The concept has its roots in J Forrester's Industrial Dynamics (1961) and thus it is also known as the Forrester Effect. Since the oscillating demand magnification upstream a supply chain reminds someone of a cracking whip it became famous as the _____.

 a. Bullwhip effect
 b. 33 Strategies of War
 c. 1990 Clean Air Act
 d. 28-hour day

15. Procter is a surname, and may also refer to:

 - Bryan Waller Procter (pseud. Barry Cornwall), English poet
 - Goodwin Procter, American law firm
 - _____, consumer products multinational

 a. Procter ' Gamble
 b. Master and Servant Acts
 c. Strict liability
 d. Downstream

16. In economics, _____ is the desire to own something and the ability to pay for it. The term _____ signifies the ability or the willingness to buy a particular commodity at a given point of time.

 a. 33 Strategies of War
 b. Demand
 c. 1990 Clean Air Act
 d. 28-hour day

17. _____ is a branch of operations research concerning itself with mathematical modeling and solution of problems concerning the placement of facilities in order to minimize transportation costs, avoid placing hazardous materials near housing, outperform competitors' facilities, etc.

Chapter 4. Supply Chain Management

A simple _____ problem is the Fermat-Weber problem, in which a single facility is to be placed, with the only optimization criterion being the minimization of the sum of distances from a given set of point sites. More complex problems considered in this discipline include the placement of multiple facilities, constraints on the locations of facilities, and more complex optimization criteria.

- a. 1990 Clean Air Act
- b. Multiscale decision making
- c. 28-hour day
- d. Facility location

18. Manufacturing Resource Planning (_____) is defined by APICS as a method for the effective planning of all resources of a manufacturing company. Ideally, it addresses operational planning in units, financial planning in dollars, and has a simulation capability to answer 'what-if' questions and extension of closed-loop MRP. Manufacturing Resource Planning (or MRP2) - Around 1980, over-frequent changes in sales forecasts, entailing continual readjustments in production, as well as the unsuitability of the parameters fixed by the system, led MRP (Material Requirement Planning) to evolve into a new concept : Manufacturing Resource Planning (e.g. MRP 2)

This is not exclusively a software function, but a marriage of people skills, dedication to data base accuracy, and computer resources.

- a. Jidoka
- b. Manufacturing resource planning
- c. Homeworkers
- d. MRP II

19. _____ is a business term which refers to a range of software tools or modules used in executing supply chain transactions, managing supplier relationships and controlling associated business processes.

While functionality in such systems can often be broad - it commonly includes:

1. Customer requirement processing
2. Purchase order processing
3. Inventory management
4. Goods receipt and Warehouse management
5. Supplier Management/Sourcing

A requirement of many _____ often includes forecasting. Such tools often attempt to balance the disparity between supply and demand by improving business processes and using algorithms and consumption analysis to better plan future needs. _____ also often includes integration technology that allows organizations to trade electronically with supply chain partners.

- a. Demand chain
- b. Supply chain management software
- c. Supply-Chain Operations Reference
- d. Vendor Managed Inventory

Chapter 4. Supply Chain Management

20. In statistics, signal processing, and many other fields, a _____ is a sequence of data points, measured typically at successive times, spaced at (often uniform) time intervals. _____ analysis comprises methods that attempt to understand such _____, often either to understand the underlying context of the data points (Where did they come from? What generated them?), or to make forecasts (predictions.) _____ forecasting is the use of a model to forecast future events based on known past events: to forecast future data points before they are measured.
   a. Moving average
   b. Histogram
   c. Standard deviation
   d. Time series

21. In statistics, signal processing, and many other fields, a time series is a sequence of data points, measured typically at successive times, spaced at (often uniform) time intervals. _____ comprises methods that attempt to understand such time series, often either to understand the underlying context of the data points (Where did they come from? What generated them?), or to make forecasts (predictions.) Time series forecasting is the use of a model to forecast future events based on known past events: to forecast future data points before they are measured.
   a. Moving average
   b. Failure rate
   c. Correlation
   d. Time series analysis

22. _____ is the process of comparing the cost, cycle time, productivity, or quality of a specific process or method to another that is widely considered to be an industry standard or best practice. Essentially, _____ provides a snapshot of the performance of your business and helps you understand where you are in relation to a particular standard. The result is often a business case for making changes in order to make improvements.
   a. Competitive heterogeneity
   b. Benchmarking
   c. Complementors
   d. Cost leadership

23. _____ is the activity of estimating the quantity of a product or service that consumers will purchase. _____ involves techniques including both informal methods, such as educated guesses, and quantitative methods, such as the use of historical sales data or current data from test markets. _____ may be used in making pricing decisions, in assessing future capacity requirements, or in making decisions on whether to enter a new market.
   a. 1990 Clean Air Act
   b. Demand Forecasting
   c. Profitability index
   d. 28-hour day

24. The term '_____' refers to the concept of collecting information and attempting to spot a pattern in the information. In some fields of study, the term '_____' has more formally-defined meanings.

   In project management _____ is a mathematical technique that uses historical results to predict future outcome.

   a. Stepwise regression
   b. Trend analysis
   c. Regression analysis
   d. Least squares

25. In business and engineering, _____ is the term used to describe the complete process of bringing a new product or service to market. There are two parallel paths involved in the _____ process: one involves the idea generation, product design, and detail engineering; the other involves market research and marketing analysis. Companies typically see _____ as the first stage in generating and commercializing new products within the overall strategic process of product life cycle management used to maintain or grow their market share.

Chapter 4. Supply Chain Management

a. New product development
b. 33 Strategies of War
c. 1990 Clean Air Act
d. 28-hour day

26. In business and engineering, new _____ is the term used to describe the complete process of bringing a new product or service to market. There are two parallel paths involved in the NProduct development process: one involves the idea generation, product design, and detail engineering; the other involves market research and marketing analysis. Companies typically see new _____ as the first stage in generating and commercializing new products within the overall strategic process of product life cycle management used to maintain or grow their market share.
a. 1990 Clean Air Act
b. Product development
c. 33 Strategies of War
d. 28-hour day

27. _____ is the use of control systems (such as numerical control, programmable logic control, and other industrial control systems), in concert with other applications of information technology (such as computer-aided technologies [CAD, CAM, CAx]), to control industrial machinery and processes, reducing the need for human intervention. In the scope of industrialization, _____ is a step beyond mechanization. Whereas mechanization provided human operators with machinery to assist them with the physical requirements of work, _____ greatly reduces the need for human sensory and mental requirements as well.
a. A4e
b. A Stake in the Outcome
c. AAAI
d. Automation

28. _____ is a joint trade and industry body working towards making the grocery sector as a whole more responsive to consumer demand and promote the removal of unnecessary costs from the supply chain.

The _____ movement beginning in the mid-nineties was characterized by the emergence of new principles of collaborative management along the supply chain. It was understood that companies can serve consumers better, faster and at less cost by working together with trading partners.

a. Event management
b. Entertainment Management
c. Efficient consumer response
d. Exception management

29. _____ consists of the sale of goods or merchandise from a fixed location, such as a department store, boutique or kiosk in small or individual lots for direct consumption by the purchaser. _____ may include subordinated services, such as delivery. Purchasers may be individuals or businesses.
a. Planogram
b. 1990 Clean Air Act
c. 28-hour day
d. Retailing

30. A _____ or business method is a collection of related, structured activities or tasks that produce a specific service or product (serve a particular goal) for a particular customer or customers. It often can be visualized with a flowchart as a sequence of activities.

Chapter 4. Supply Chain Management

There are three types of _____ es:

1. Management processes, the processes that govern the operation of a system. Typical management processes include 'Corporate Governance' and 'Strategic Management'.
2. Operational processes, processes that constitute the core business and create the primary value stream. Typical operational processes are Purchasing, Manufacturing, Marketing, and Sales.
3. Supporting processes, which support the core processes. Examples include Accounting, Recruitment, Technical support.

A _____ begins with a customer's need and ends with a customer's need fulfillment. Process oriented organizations break down the barriers of structural departments and try to avoid functional silos.

  a. 28-hour day
  c. 1990 Clean Air Act
  b. 33 Strategies of War
  d. Business process

31. _____ is, in very basic words, a position a firm occupies against its competitors.

According to Michael Porter, the three methods for creating a sustainable _____ are through:

1. Cost leadership

2. Differentiation

3. Focus (economics)

  a. Theory Z
  c. Competitive advantage
  b. 1990 Clean Air Act
  d. 28-hour day

32. _____ is a broad label that refers to any individuals or households that use goods and services generated within the economy. The concept of a _____ is used in different contexts, so that the usage and significance of the term may vary.

Typically when business people and economists talk of _____ s they are talking about person as _____ , an aggregated commodity item with little individuality other than that expressed in the buy/not-buy decision.

  a. 28-hour day
  c. Consumer
  b. 1990 Clean Air Act
  d. 33 Strategies of War

33. _____ refers to the structured transmission of data between organizations by electronic means. It is used to transfer electronic documents from one computer system to another (ie) from one trading partner to another trading partner. It is more than mere E-mail; for instance, organizations might replace bills of lading and even checks with appropriate _____ messages.

Chapter 4. Supply Chain Management

a. AAAI
b. A4e
c. A Stake in the Outcome
d. Electronic data interchange

34. _____, in microeconomics, are the cost advantages that a business obtains due to expansion. They are factors that cause a producer's average cost per unit to fall as scale is increased. _____ is a long run concept and refers to reductions in unit cost as the size of a facility, or scale, increases.
   a. Economies of scale
   b. A Stake in the Outcome
   c. Economies of scope
   d. A4e

35. _____ describes commerce transactions between businesses, such as between a manufacturer and a wholesaler, or between a wholesaler and a retailer. Contrasting terms are business-to-consumer (B2C) and business-to-government (B2G.)

The volume of B2B transactions is much higher than the volume of B2C transactions.

   a. Product bundling
   b. Business-to-business
   c. Market environment
   d. Category management

36. In economics, business, retail, and accounting, a _____ is the value of money that has been used up to produce something, and hence is not available for use anymore. In economics, a _____ is an alternative that is given up as a result of a decision. In business, the _____ may be one of acquisition, in which case the amount of money expended to acquire it is counted as _____.
   a. Cost allocation
   b. Cost
   c. Fixed costs
   d. Cost overrun

37. _____ is one of the four elements of marketing mix. An organization or set of organizations (go-betweens) involved in the process of making a product or service available for use or consumption by a consumer or business user.

The other three parts of the marketing mix are product, pricing, and promotion.

   a. Job creation programs
   b. Matching theory
   c. Missing completely at random
   d. Distribution

38. In economics, _____ is the removal of intermediaries in a supply chain: 'cutting out the middleman'. Instead of going through traditional distribution channels, which had some type of intermediate (such as a distributor, wholesaler, broker, or agent), companies may now deal with every customer directly, for example via the Internet. One important factor is a drop in the cost of servicing customers directly.
   a. 1990 Clean Air Act
   b. 28-hour day
   c. Disintermediation
   d. Virtual enterprise

39. A _____ for a set of products is a warehouse or other specialized building, often with refrigeration or air conditioning, which is stocked with products (goods) to be re-distributed to retailers, wholesalers or directly to consumers. A _____ is a principle part, the 'order processing' element, of the entire 'order fulfillment' process. _____s are usually thought of as being 'demand driven'.

Chapter 4. Supply Chain Management

a. 28-hour day
b. Distribution center
c. 1990 Clean Air Act
d. Third-party logistics

40. A _____ is an entity formed between two or more parties to undertake economic activity together. The parties agree to create a new entity by both contributing equity, and they then share in the revenues, expenses, and control of the enterprise. The venture can be for one specific project only, or a continuing business relationship such as the Fuji Xerox _____.

a. Patent
b. Meritor Savings Bank v. Vinson
c. Joint venture
d. Civil Rights Act of 1991

41. An _____ is a person who has possession of an enterprise and assumes significant accountability for the inherent risks and the outcome. It is an ambitious leader who combines land, labor, and capital to create and market new goods or services. The term is a loanword from French and was first defined by the Irish economist Richard Cantillon.

a. AAAI
b. Entrepreneur
c. A Stake in the Outcome
d. A4e

Chapter 5. Integrating Manufacturing and Services

1. _____ is the use of control systems (such as numerical control, programmable logic control, and other industrial control systems), in concert with other applications of information technology (such as computer-aided technologies [CAD, CAM, CAx]), to control industrial machinery and processes, reducing the need for human intervention. In the scope of industrialization, _____ is a step beyond mechanization. Whereas mechanization provided human operators with machinery to assist them with the physical requirements of work, _____ greatly reduces the need for human sensory and mental requirements as well.

   a. A4e
   b. A Stake in the Outcome
   c. AAAI
   d. Automation

2. _____ is a branch of operations research concerning itself with mathematical modeling and solution of problems concerning the placement of facilities in order to minimize transportation costs, avoid placing hazardous materials near housing, outperform competitors' facilities, etc.

   A simple _____ problem is the Fermat-Weber problem, in which a single facility is to be placed, with the only optimization criterion being the minimization of the sum of distances from a given set of point sites. More complex problems considered in this discipline include the placement of multiple facilities, constraints on the locations of facilities, and more complex optimization criteria.

   a. Multiscale decision making
   b. Facility location
   c. 28-hour day
   d. 1990 Clean Air Act

3. The _____ is a trilateral trade bloc in North America created by the governments of the United States, Canada, and Mexico. The agreement creating the trade bloc came into force on January 1, 1994. It superseded the Canada-United States Free Trade Agreement between the U.S. and Canada.

   a. North American Free Trade Agreement
   b. Trade union
   c. Business war game
   d. Career portfolios

4. _____ is an advertisement in which a particular product specifically mentions a competitor by name for the express purpose of showing why the competitor is inferior to the product naming it.

   This should not be confused with parody advertisements, where a fictional product is being advertised for the purpose of poking fun at the particular advertisement, nor should it be confused with the use of a coined brand name for the purpose of comparing the product without actually naming an actual competitor. ('Wikipedia tastes better and is less filling than the Encyclopedia Galactica.')

   In the 1980s, during what has been referred to as the cola wars, soft-drink manufacturer Pepsi ran a series of advertisements where people, caught on hidden camera, in a blind taste test, chose Pepsi over rival Coca-Cola.

   a. 28-hour day
   b. 33 Strategies of War
   c. 1990 Clean Air Act
   d. Comparative advertising

5. _____ refers to the difference between the cost of materials purchased by a company plus the cost of the labor to assemble a product and the price at which the company sells the product. An example is the price of gasoline at the pump over the price of the oil in it. In national accounts used in macroeconomics, it refers to the contribution of the factors of production, i.e., land, labor, and capital goods, to raising the value of a product and corresponds to the incomes received by the owners of these factors.

a. Deregulation
b. Minimum wage
c. Rehn-Meidner Model
d. Value added

6. A _____ is popular as a telecommunications industry term for non-core services or, in short, all services beyond standard voice calls and fax transmissions but, it can be used in ANY service industry (eg. Web 2.0) for the services providers provide for no cost to promote their main service business. In telecommunication industry on a conceptual level, _____s add value to the standard service offering, spurring the subscriber to use their phone more and allowing the operator to drive up their ARPU.

a. Value-added service
b. 33 Strategies of War
c. 1990 Clean Air Act
d. 28-hour day

7. _____ is the process of comparing the cost, cycle time, productivity, or quality of a specific process or method to another that is widely considered to be an industry standard or best practice. Essentially, _____ provides a snapshot of the performance of your business and helps you understand where you are in relation to a particular standard. The result is often a business case for making changes in order to make improvements.

a. Competitive heterogeneity
b. Cost leadership
c. Complementors
d. Benchmarking

8. _____ is understood as a business unit within the overall corporate identity which is distinguishable from other business because it serves a defined external market where management can conduct strategic planning in relation to products and markets. When companies become really large, they are best thought of as being composed of a number of businesses (or _____s.)

In the broader domain of strategic management, the phrase '_____' came into use in the 1960s, largely as a result of General Electric's many units.

a. Strategic drift
b. Strategic group
c. Switching cost
d. Strategic business unit

9. _____, a business term, is a measure of how products and services supplied by a company meet or surpass customer expectation. It is seen as a key performance indicator within business and is part of the four perspectives of a Balanced Scorecard.

In a competitive marketplace where businesses compete for customers, _____ is seen as a key differentiator and increasingly has become a key element of business strategy.

a. Horizontal integration
b. Foreign ownership
c. Critical Success Factor
d. Customer satisfaction

10. The _____, is a mathematically based algorithm for scheduling a set of project activities. It is an important tool for effective project management.

It was developed in the 1950s by the Dupont Corporation at about the same time that General Dynamics and the US Navy were developing the Program Evaluation and Review Technique (PERT) Today, it is commonly used with all forms of projects, including construction, software development, research projects, product development, engineering, and plant maintenance, among others.

Chapter 5. Integrating Manufacturing and Services

a. 1990 Clean Air Act
b. 33 Strategies of War
c. 28-hour day
d. Critical Path Method

11. _____ in manufacturing refers to processes that occur later on in a production sequence or production line.

Viewing a company 'from order to cash' might have high-level processes such as Marketing, Sales, Order Entry, Manufacturing, Packaging, Shipping, Invoicing. Each of these could be deconstructed into many sub-processes and supporting processes.

a. Science Learning Centre
b. Probability-generating function
c. Downstream
d. Genbutsu

12. _____ is the provision of service to customers before, during and after a purchase.

According to Turban et al. (2002), '_____ is a series of activities designed to enhance the level of customer satisfaction - that is, the feeling that a product or service has met the customer expectation.'

Its importance varies by product, industry and customer; defective or broken merchandise can be exchanged, often only with a receipt and within a specified time frame.

a. 1990 Clean Air Act
b. Service rate
c. Customer service
d. 28-hour day

13. Manufacturing Resource Planning (_____) is defined by APICS as a method for the effective planning of all resources of a manufacturing company. Ideally, it addresses operational planning in units, financial planning in dollars, and has a simulation capability to answer 'what-if' questions and extension of closed-loop MRP. Manufacturing Resource Planning (or MRP2) - Around 1980, over-frequent changes in sales forecasts, entailing continual readjustments in production, as well as the unsuitability of the parameters fixed by the system, led MRP (Material Requirement Planning) to evolve into a new concept : Manufacturing Resource Planning (e.g. MRP 2)

This is not exclusively a software function, but a marriage of people skills, dedication to data base accuracy, and computer resources.

a. Homeworkers
b. MRP II
c. Manufacturing resource planning
d. Jidoka

14. A _____ or business method is a collection of related, structured activities or tasks that produce a specific service or product (serve a particular goal) for a particular customer or customers. It often can be visualized with a flowchart as a sequence of activities.

There are three types of _____es:

1. Management processes, the processes that govern the operation of a system. Typical management processes include 'Corporate Governance' and 'Strategic Management'.
2. Operational processes, processes that constitute the core business and create the primary value stream. Typical operational processes are Purchasing, Manufacturing, Marketing, and Sales.
3. Supporting processes, which support the core processes. Examples include Accounting, Recruitment, Technical support.

A _____ begins with a customer's need and ends with a customer's need fulfillment. Process oriented organizations break down the barriers of structural departments and try to avoid functional silos.

- a. 1990 Clean Air Act
- b. 28-hour day
- c. Business process
- d. 33 Strategies of War

15. _____ consists of the sale of goods or merchandise from a fixed location, such as a department store, boutique or kiosk in small or individual lots for direct consumption by the purchaser. _____ may include subordinated services, such as delivery. Purchasers may be individuals or businesses.

- a. Planogram
- b. 1990 Clean Air Act
- c. 28-hour day
- d. Retailing

Chapter 6. New Product and Service Development, and Process Selection

1. _____ is the largest book retailer in the United States, operating mainly through its Barnes ' Noble Booksellers chain of bookstores headquartered in lower Fifth Avenue in Manhattan.

The company operates the chain of small 'B.

a. 28-hour day
b. 33 Strategies of War
c. Barnes ' Noble, Inc.
d. 1990 Clean Air Act

2. _____ is an advertisement in which a particular product specifically mentions a competitor by name for the express purpose of showing why the competitor is inferior to the product naming it.

This should not be confused with parody advertisements, where a fictional product is being advertised for the purpose of poking fun at the particular advertisement, nor should it be confused with the use of a coined brand name for the purpose of comparing the product without actually naming an actual competitor. ('Wikipedia tastes better and is less filling than the Encyclopedia Galactica.')

In the 1980s, during what has been referred to as the cola wars, soft-drink manufacturer Pepsi ran a series of advertisements where people, caught on hidden camera, in a blind taste test, chose Pepsi over rival Coca-Cola.

a. 33 Strategies of War
b. 1990 Clean Air Act
c. 28-hour day
d. Comparative advertising

3. _____ is the process of comparing the cost, cycle time, productivity, or quality of a specific process or method to another that is widely considered to be an industry standard or best practice. Essentially, _____ provides a snapshot of the performance of your business and helps you understand where you are in relation to a particular standard. The result is often a business case for making changes in order to make improvements.

a. Cost leadership
b. Competitive heterogeneity
c. Complementors
d. Benchmarking

4. _____, in microeconomics, are the cost advantages that a business obtains due to expansion. They are factors that cause a producer's average cost per unit to fall as scale is increased. _____ is a long run concept and refers to reductions in unit cost as the size of a facility, or scale, increases.

a. A Stake in the Outcome
b. Economies of scale
c. A4e
d. Economies of scope

5. _____ is the use of control systems (such as numerical control, programmable logic control, and other industrial control systems), in concert with other applications of information technology (such as computer-aided technologies [CAD, CAM, CAx]), to control industrial machinery and processes, reducing the need for human intervention. In the scope of industrialization, _____ is a step beyond mechanization. Whereas mechanization provided human operators with machinery to assist them with the physical requirements of work, _____ greatly reduces the need for human sensory and mental requirements as well.

a. AAAI
b. A Stake in the Outcome
c. A4e
d. Automation

6. _____ is a branch of operations research concerning itself with mathematical modeling and solution of problems concerning the placement of facilities in order to minimize transportation costs, avoid placing hazardous materials near housing, outperform competitors' facilities, etc.

Chapter 6. New Product and Service Development, and Process Selection

A simple _____ problem is the Fermat-Weber problem, in which a single facility is to be placed, with the only optimization criterion being the minimization of the sum of distances from a given set of point sites. More complex problems considered in this discipline include the placement of multiple facilities, constraints on the locations of facilities, and more complex optimization criteria.

a. Facility location
b. Multiscale decision making
c. 28-hour day
d. 1990 Clean Air Act

7. _____ is the management of the flow of goods, information and other resources, including energy and people, between the point of origin and the point of consumption in order to meet the requirements of consumers (frequently, and originally, military organizations.) _____ involves the integration of information, transportation, inventory, warehousing, material-handling, and packaging, and occasionally security. _____ is a channel of the supply chain which adds the value of time and place utility.

a. 28-hour day
b. Third-party logistics
c. 1990 Clean Air Act
d. Logistics

8. The _____ is a trilateral trade bloc in North America created by the governments of the United States, Canada, and Mexico. The agreement creating the trade bloc came into force on January 1, 1994. It superseded the Canada-United States Free Trade Agreement between the U.S. and Canada.

a. Career portfolios
b. Trade union
c. Business war game
d. North American Free Trade Agreement

9. In business and engineering, _____ is the term used to describe the complete process of bringing a new product or service to market. There are two parallel paths involved in the _____ process: one involves the idea generation, product design, and detail engineering; the other involves market research and marketing analysis. Companies typically see _____ as the first stage in generating and commercializing new products within the overall strategic process of product life cycle management used to maintain or grow their market share.

a. 28-hour day
b. New product development
c. 1990 Clean Air Act
d. 33 Strategies of War

10. _____ is the automatic construction of physical objects using solid freeform fabrication. The first techniques for _____ became available in the late 1980s and were used to produce models and prototype parts. Today, they are used for a much wider range of applications and are even used to manufacture production quality parts in relatively small numbers.

a. 28-hour day
b. 1990 Clean Air Act
c. 33 Strategies of War
d. Rapid prototyping

11. An _____ is a manufacturing process in which parts (usually interchangeable parts) are added to a product in a sequential manner using optimally planned logistics to create a finished product much faster than with handcrafting-type methods. The _____ developed by Ford Motor Company between 1908 and 1915 made _____s famous in the following decade through the social ramifications of mass production, such as the affordability of the Ford Model T and the introduction of high wages for Ford workers. However, the various preconditions for the development at Ford stretched far back into the 19th century, from the gradual realization of the dream of interchangeability, to the concept of reinventing workflow and job descriptions using analytical methods.

Chapter 6. New Product and Service Development, and Process Selection

a. A Stake in the Outcome
b. Assembly line
c. A4e
d. AAAI

12. A _____ or business method is a collection of related, structured activities or tasks that produce a specific service or product (serve a particular goal) for a particular customer or customers. It often can be visualized with a flowchart as a sequence of activities.

There are three types of _____es:

1. Management processes, the processes that govern the operation of a system. Typical management processes include 'Corporate Governance' and 'Strategic Management'.
2. Operational processes, processes that constitute the core business and create the primary value stream. Typical operational processes are Purchasing, Manufacturing, Marketing, and Sales.
3. Supporting processes, which support the core processes. Examples include Accounting, Recruitment, Technical support.

A _____ begins with a customer's need and ends with a customer's need fulfillment. Process oriented organizations break down the barriers of structural departments and try to avoid functional silos.

a. 33 Strategies of War
b. 28-hour day
c. 1990 Clean Air Act
d. Business process

13. _____ is, in very basic words, a position a firm occupies against its competitors.

According to Michael Porter, the three methods for creating a sustainable _____ are through:

1. Cost leadership

2. Differentiation

3. Focus (economics)

a. Competitive advantage
b. 28-hour day
c. Theory Z
d. 1990 Clean Air Act

14. In business and engineering, new _____ is the term used to describe the complete process of bringing a new product or service to market. There are two parallel paths involved in the NProduct development process: one involves the idea generation, product design, and detail engineering; the other involves market research and marketing analysis. Companies typically see new _____ as the first stage in generating and commercializing new products within the overall strategic process of product life cycle management used to maintain or grow their market share.
a. Product development
b. 1990 Clean Air Act
c. 33 Strategies of War
d. 28-hour day

Chapter 6. New Product and Service Development, and Process Selection

15. A _____ is a general term that describes any government policy or regulation that restricts international trade. The barriers can take many forms, including the following terms that include many restrictions in international trade within multiple countries that import and export any items of trade.

- Import duty
- Import licenses
- Export licenses
- Import quotas
- Tariffs
- Subsidies
- Non-tariff barriers to trade
- Voluntary Export Restraints
- Local Content Requirements
- Embargo

Most _____s work on the same principle: the imposition of some sort of cost on trade that raises the price of the traded products. If two or more nations repeatedly use _____s against each other, then a trade war results.

a. Most favoured nation
c. Customs brokerage

b. Trade creation
d. Trade barrier

16. _____ is an integrated communications-based process through which individuals and communities discover that existing and newly-identified needs and wants may be satisfied by the products and services of others.

_____ is defined by the American _____ Association as the activity, set of institutions, and processes for creating, communicating, delivering, and exchanging offerings that have value for customers, clients, partners, and society at large. The term developed from the original meaning which referred literally to going to market, as in shopping, or going to a market to buy or sell goods or services.

a. Customer relationship management
c. Marketing

b. Market development
d. Disruptive technology

17. _____ is a work methodology based on the parallelization of tasks (ie. concurrently.) It refers to an approach used in product development in which functions of design engineering, manufacturing engineering and other functions are integrated to reduce the elapsed time required to bring a new product to the market.

a. Project management
c. Critical Chain Project Management

b. Concurrent engineering
d. Work package

18. _____ is the provision of service to customers before, during and after a purchase.

According to Turban et al. (2002), '_____ is a series of activities designed to enhance the level of customer satisfaction - that is, the feeling that a product or service has met the customer expectation.'

Its importance varies by product, industry and customer; defective or broken merchandise can be exchanged, often only with a receipt and within a specified time frame.

Chapter 6. New Product and Service Development, and Process Selection

a. Customer service
b. Service rate
c. 1990 Clean Air Act
d. 28-hour day

19. Marketing research is a form of business research and is generally divided into two categories: consumer _____ and business-to-business (B2B) _____, which was previously known as industrial marketing research. Consumer marketing research studies the buying habits of individual people while business-to-business marketing research investigates the markets for products sold by one business to another.

Consumer _____ is a form of applied sociology that concentrates on understanding the behaviours, whims and preferences, of consumers in a market-based economy, and aims to understand the effects and comparative success of marketing campaigns.

a. Questionnaire construction
b. Mystery shoppers
c. Questionnaire
d. Market research

20. _____ is a 'method to transform user demands into design quality, to deploy the functions forming quality, and to deploy methods for achieving the design quality into subsystems and component parts, and ultimately to specific elements of the manufacturing process.' , as described by Dr. Yoji Akao, who originally developed _____ in Japan in 1966, when the author combined his work in quality assurance and quality control points with function deployment used in Value Engineering.

_____ is designed to help planners focus on characteristics of a new or existing product or service from the viewpoints of market segments, company, or technology-development needs. The technique yields graphs and matrices.

a. 1990 Clean Air Act
b. Hoshin Kanri
c. Learning organization
d. Quality function deployment

21. _____ is a graphic tool for defining the relationship between customer desires and the firm/product capabilities. It is a part of the Quality Function Deployment (QFD) and it utilizes a planning matrix to relate what the customer wants to how a firm (that produce the products) is going to meet those wants. It looks like a House with correlation matrix as its roof, customer wants versus product features as the main part, competitor evaluation as the porch etc.

a. Consensus-seeking decision-making
b. House of quality
c. Health management system
d. Decision Matrix

22. _____ or lean production, which is often known simply as 'Lean', is a production practice that considers the expenditure of resources for any goal other than the creation of value for the end customer to be wasteful, and thus a target for elimination. Working from the perspective of the customer who consumes a product or service, 'value' is defined as any action or process that a customer would be willing to pay for. Basically, lean is centered around creating more value with less work.

a. Production line
b. Theory of constraints
c. Lean manufacturing
d. Six Sigma

Chapter 6. New Product and Service Development, and Process Selection

23. _____ consists of the mental process of thinking involved with the process of judging the merits of multiple options and selecting one of them for action. Some simple examples include deciding whether to get up in the morning or go back to sleep, or selecting a given route for a journey. More complex examples (often decisions that affect what a person thinks or their core beliefs) include choosing a lifestyle, religious affiliation, or political position.
   a. Trade study
   b. Groups decision making
   c. Choice
   d. Championship mobilization

24. _____ is a recursive process where two or more people or organizations work together in an intersection of common goals -- for example, an intellectual endeavor that is creative in nature--by sharing knowledge, learning and building consensus. _____ does not require leadership and can sometimes bring better results through decentralization and egalitarianism. In particular, teams that work collaboratively can obtain greater resources, recognition and reward when facing competition for finite resources. _____ is also present in opposing goals exhibiting the notion of adversarial _____, though this is not a common case for using the term.
   a. 1990 Clean Air Act
   b. 28-hour day
   c. Collectivism
   d. Collaboration

25. _____ is an inventory strategy that strives to improve the return on investment of a business by reducing in-process inventory and its associated carrying costs. To meet _____ objectives, the process relies on signals between different points in the process. This means the process is often driven by a series of signals, or Kanban, which tell production when to make the next part. Kanban are usually 'tickets' but can be simple visual signals, such as the presence or absence of a part on a shelf. Implemented correctly, _____ can dramatically improve a manufacturing organization's return on investment, quality, and efficiency.
   a. 33 Strategies of War
   b. 28-hour day
   c. Just-in-time
   d. 1990 Clean Air Act

26. _____ is used for the design, development, analysis, and optimization of technical processes and is mainly applied to chemical plants and chemical processes, but also to power stations, and similar technical facilities. Process flow diagram of a typical amine treating process used in industrial plants

   _____ is a model-based representation of chemical, physical, biological, and other technical processes and unit operations in software. Basic prerequisites are a thorough knowledge of chemical and physical properties of pure components and mixtures, of reactions, and of mathematical models which, in combination, allow the calculation of a process in computers.

   a. 1990 Clean Air Act
   b. Process simulation
   c. 28-hour day
   d. 33 Strategies of War

Chapter 6. New Product and Service Development, and Process Selection

27. _____ refers to the movement of cash into or out of a business or financial product. It is usually measured during a specified, finite period of time. Measurement of _____ can be used

- to determine a project's rate of return or value. The time of _____s into and out of projects are used as inputs in financial models such as internal rate of return, and net present value.
- to determine problems with a business's liquidity. Being profitable does not necessarily mean being liquid. A company can fail because of a shortage of cash, even while profitable.
- as an alternate measure of a business's profits when it is believed that accrual accounting concepts do not represent economic realities. For example, a company may be notionally profitable but generating little operational cash (as may be the case for a company that barters its products rather than selling for cash.) In such a case, the company may be deriving additional operating cash by issuing shares evaluating default risk, re-investment requirements, etc.

_____ is a generic term used differently depending on the context. It may be defined by users for their own purposes.

   a. Cash flow
   c. Sweat equity
   b. Gross profit
   d. Gross profit margin

28. _____ are typically small manufacturing operations that handle specialized manufacturing processes such as small customer orders or small batch jobs. _____ typically move on to different jobs (possibly with different customers) when each job is completed. By nature of this type of manufacturing operation, _____ are usually specialized in skill and processes.
   a. 1990 Clean Air Act
   c. 33 Strategies of War
   b. Job shops
   d. 28-hour day

29. _____ is one of the managerial functions like planning, organizing, staffing and directing. It is an important function because it helps to check the errors and to take the corrective action so that deviation from standards are minimized and stated goals of the organization are achieved in desired manner. According to modern concepts, _____ is a foreseeing action whereas earlier concept of _____ was used only when errors were detected. _____ in management means setting standards, measuring actual performance and taking corrective action.
   a. Decision tree pruning
   c. Schedule of reinforcement
   b. Turnover
   d. Control

30. In probability theory, a probability distribution is called _____ if its cumulative distribution function is _____. This is equivalent to saying that for random variables X with the distribution in question, Pr[X = a] = 0 for all real numbers a, i.e.: the probability that X attains the value a is zero, for any number a. If the distribution of X is _____ then X is called a _____ random variable.
   a. Decision tree pruning
   c. Pay Band
   b. Connectionist expert systems
   d. Continuous

31. A _____ is a set of sequential operations established in a factory whereby materials are put through a refining process to produce an end-product that is suitable for onward consumption; or components are assembled to make a finished article.

Typically, raw materials such as metal ores or agricultural products such as foodstuffs or textile source plants (cotton, flax) require a sequence of treatments to render them useful. For metal, the processes include crushing, smelting and further refining.

a. Theory of constraints
b. Six Sigma
c. Takt time
d. Production line

32. _____, a business term, is a measure of how products and services supplied by a company meet or surpass customer expectation. It is seen as a key performance indicator within business and is part of the four perspectives of a Balanced Scorecard.

In a competitive marketplace where businesses compete for customers, _____ is seen as a key differentiator and increasingly has become a key element of business strategy.

a. Horizontal integration
b. Critical Success Factor
c. Customer satisfaction
d. Foreign ownership

Chapter 7. Project Management

1. _____ is an advertisement in which a particular product specifically mentions a competitor by name for the express purpose of showing why the competitor is inferior to the product naming it.

This should not be confused with parody advertisements, where a fictional product is being advertised for the purpose of poking fun at the particular advertisement, nor should it be confused with the use of a coined brand name for the purpose of comparing the product without actually naming an actual competitor. ('Wikipedia tastes better and is less filling than the Encyclopedia Galactica.')

In the 1980s, during what has been referred to as the cola wars, soft-drink manufacturer Pepsi ran a series of advertisements where people, caught on hidden camera, in a blind taste test, chose Pepsi over rival Coca-Cola.

  a. 28-hour day
  c. 33 Strategies of War
  b. 1990 Clean Air Act
  d. Comparative advertising

2. The Program (or Project) Evaluation and Review Technique, commonly abbreviated _____, is a model for project management designed to analyze and represent the tasks involved in completing a given project.

_____ is a method to analyze the involved tasks in completing a given project, specially the time needed to complete each task, and identifying the minimum time needed to complete the total project.

_____ was developed primarily to simplify the planning and scheduling of large and complex projects.

  a. 28-hour day
  c. 33 Strategies of War
  b. 1990 Clean Air Act
  d. PERT

3. _____ refers to the movement of cash into or out of a business or financial product. It is usually measured during a specified, finite period of time. Measurement of _____ can be used

- to determine a project's rate of return or value. The time of _____s into and out of projects are used as inputs in financial models such as internal rate of return, and net present value.
- to determine problems with a business's liquidity. Being profitable does not necessarily mean being liquid. A company can fail because of a shortage of cash, even while profitable.
- as an alternate measure of a business's profits when it is believed that accrual accounting concepts do not represent economic realities. For example, a company may be notionally profitable but generating little operational cash (as may be the case for a company that barters its products rather than selling for cash.) In such a case, the company may be deriving additional operating cash by issuing shares evaluating default risk, re-investment requirements, etc.

_____ is a generic term used differently depending on the context. It may be defined by users for their own purposes.

  a. Gross profit
  c. Sweat equity
  b. Cash flow
  d. Gross profit margin

4. _____ is the discipline of planning, organizing and managing resources to bring about the successful completion of specific project goals and objectives. It is often closely related to and sometimes conflated with Program management.

Chapter 7. Project Management

A project is a finite endeavor--having specific start and completion dates--undertaken to meet particular goals and objectives, usually to bring about beneficial change or added value.

  a. Work package
  b. Project engineer
  c. Precedence diagram
  d. Project management

5. A _____ is a document that captures and agrees the work activities, deliverables and timeline that a vendor will execute against in performance of work for a customer. Detailed requirements and pricing are usually specified in a _____, along with many other terms and conditions.

There are many formats and styles of _____ document templates that have been specialized for the Hardware or Software solutions being described in the Request for Proposal.

  a. 28-hour day
  b. Modular design
  c. Statement of work
  d. 1990 Clean Air Act

6. _____ is one of the managerial functions like planning, organizing, staffing and directing. It is an important function because it helps to check the errors and to take the corrective action so that deviation from standards are minimized and stated goals of the organization are achieved in desired manner. According to modern concepts, _____ is a foreseeing action whereas earlier concept of _____ was used only when errors were detected. _____ in management means setting standards, measuring actual performance and taking corrective action.

  a. Schedule of reinforcement
  b. Decision tree pruning
  c. Turnover
  d. Control

7. A _____ in project management and systems engineering, is a tool used to define and group a project's discrete work elements (or tasks) in a way that helps organize and define the total work scope of the project.

A _____ element may be a product, data, a service, or any combination. A _____ also provides the necessary framework for detailed cost estimating and control along with providing guidance for schedule development and control.

  a. 28-hour day
  b. 1990 Clean Air Act
  c. 33 Strategies of War
  d. Work breakdown structure

8. In business and engineering, _____ is the term used to describe the complete process of bringing a new product or service to market. There are two parallel paths involved in the _____ process: one involves the idea generation, product design, and detail engineering; the other involves market research and marketing analysis. Companies typically see _____ as the first stage in generating and commercializing new products within the overall strategic process of product life cycle management used to maintain or grow their market share.

  a. 28-hour day
  b. 1990 Clean Air Act
  c. New product development
  d. 33 Strategies of War

9. A _____ is a professional in the field of project management. _____s can have the responsibility of the planning, execution, and closing of any project, typically relating to construction industry, architecture, computer networking, telecommunications or software development.

Chapter 7. Project Management

Many other fields in the production, design and service industries also have _____s.

a. Project engineer
c. Project management
b. Work package
d. Project manager

10. _____ is a process of planning and controlling the performance or execution of any type of activity, such as:

- a project (project _____) or
- a process (process _____, sometimes referred to as the process performance measurement and management system.)

Organization's senior management is responsible for carrying out its _____.

a. Participatory management
c. Management process
b. Work design
d. Human Relations Movement

11. In business and engineering, new _____ is the term used to describe the complete process of bringing a new product or service to market. There are two parallel paths involved in the NProduct development process: one involves the idea generation, product design, and detail engineering; the other involves market research and marketing analysis. Companies typically see new _____ as the first stage in generating and commercializing new products within the overall strategic process of product life cycle management used to maintain or grow their market share.

a. 1990 Clean Air Act
c. 33 Strategies of War
b. Product development
d. 28-hour day

12. _____ can be considered to have three main components: quality control, quality assurance and quality improvement. _____ is focused not only on product quality, but also the means to achieve it. _____ therefore uses quality assurance and control of processes as well as products to achieve more consistent quality.

a. 28-hour day
c. Quality management
b. Total quality management
d. 1990 Clean Air Act

13. _____ is a business management strategy aimed at embedding awareness of quality in all organizational processes. _____ has been widely used in manufacturing, education, hospitals, call centers, government, and service industries, as well as NASA space and science programs.

As defined by the International Organization for Standardization (ISO):

'_____ is a management approach for an organization, centered on quality, based on the participation of all its members and aiming at long-term success through customer satisfaction, and benefits to all members of the organization and to society.' ISO 8402:1994

One major aim is to reduce variation from every process so that greater consistency of effort is obtained. (Royse, D., Thyer, B., Padgett D., ' Logan T., 2006)

Chapter 7. Project Management

a. 1990 Clean Air Act
b. 28-hour day
c. Quality management
d. Total quality management

14. In organizational development (OD), _____ is the application of Socio-Technical Systems principles and techniques to the humanization of work.

The aims of _____ to improved job satisfaction, to improved through-put, to improved quality and to reduced employee problems, e.g., grievances, absenteeism.

Under scientific management people would be directed by reason and the problems of industrial unrest would be appropriately (i.e., scientifically) addressed.

a. Management process
b. Path-goal theory
c. Graduate recruitment
d. Work design

15. A _____ is a type of bar chart that illustrates a project schedule. _____s illustrate the start and finish dates of the terminal elements and summary elements of a project. Terminal elements and summary elements comprise the work breakdown structure of the project.

a. 28-hour day
b. Gantt chart
c. 33 Strategies of War
d. 1990 Clean Air Act

16. A _____ is a plan for production, staffing, inventory, etc. It is usually linked to manufacturing where the plan indicates when and how much of each product will be demanded. This plan quantifies significant processes, parts, and other resources in order to optimize production, to identify bottlenecks, and to anticipate needs and completed goods.

a. Remanufacturing
b. Piecework
c. Value engineering
d. Master production schedule

17. The _____, is a mathematically based algorithm for scheduling a set of project activities. It is an important tool for effective project management.

It was developed in the 1950s by the Dupont Corporation at about the same time that General Dynamics and the US Navy were developing the Program Evaluation and Review Technique (PERT) Today, it is commonly used with all forms of projects, including construction, software development, research projects, product development, engineering, and plant maintenance, among others.

a. 28-hour day
b. 33 Strategies of War
c. 1990 Clean Air Act
d. Critical Path Method

18. In economics, business, retail, and accounting, a _____ is the value of money that has been used up to produce something, and hence is not available for use anymore. In economics, a _____ is an alternative that is given up as a result of a decision. In business, the _____ may be one of acquisition, in which case the amount of money expended to acquire it is counted as _____.

a. Fixed costs
b. Cost overrun
c. Cost allocation
d. Cost

Chapter 7. Project Management

19. _____ is a costing model that identifies activities in an organization and assigns the cost of each activity resource to all products and services according to the actual consumption by each: it assigns more indirect costs (overhead) into direct costs.

In this way an organization can establish the true cost of its individual products and services for the purposes of identifying and eliminating those which are unprofitable and lowering the prices of those which are overpriced.

In a business organization, the ABC methodology assigns an organization's resource costs through activities to the products and services provided to its customers.

a. A Stake in the Outcome
b. Activity-based costing
c. A4e
d. Indirect costs

20. _____ of the learning curve effect and the closely related experience curve effect express the relationship between equations for experience and efficiency or between efficiency gains and investment in the effort. The experience of 'learning curves' was first observed by the 19th Century German psychologist Hermann Ebbinghaus according to the difficulty of memorizing varying numbers of verbal stimuli, and subsequent learning about the complex processes of learning are discussed in the

.

The rule used for representing the learning curve effect states that the more times a task has been performed, the less time will be required on each subsequent iteration.

a. Spatial Decision Support Systems
b. Point biserial correlation coefficient
c. Distribution
d. Models

21. _____ is a method of planning and managing projects that puts the main emphasis on the resources required to execute project tasks. It was developed by Eliyahu M. Goldratt. This is in contrast to the more traditional Critical Path and PERT methods, which emphasize task order and rigid scheduling. A Critical Chain project network will tend to keep the resources levelly loaded, but will require them to be flexible in their start times and to quickly switch between tasks and task chains to keep the whole project on schedule.

a. Precedence diagram
b. Project management office
c. Critical Chain Project Management
d. Project engineer

22. Manufacturing Resource Planning (_____) is defined by APICS as a method for the effective planning of all resources of a manufacturing company. Ideally, it addresses operational planning in units, financial planning in dollars, and has a simulation capability to answer 'what-if' questions and extension of closed-loop MRP. Manufacturing Resource Planning (or MRP2) - Around 1980, over-frequent changes in sales forecasts, entailing continual readjustments in production, as well as the unsuitability of the parameters fixed by the system, led MRP (Material Requirement Planning) to evolve into a new concept : Manufacturing Resource Planning (e.g. MRP 2)

This is not exclusively a software function, but a marriage of people skills, dedication to data base accuracy, and computer resources.

a. Manufacturing resource planning
b. MRP II
c. Homeworkers
d. Jidoka

23. The _____ of 1985 is a law passed by the U.S. Congress and signed by President Reagan that, among other things, mandates an insurance program giving some employees the ability to continue health insurance coverage after leaving employment. _____ includes amendments to the Employee Retirement Income Security Act of 1974 (ERISA.) The law deals with a great variety of subjects, such as tobacco price supports, railroads, private pension plans, disability insurance, and the postal service, but it is perhaps best known for Title X, which amends the Internal Revenue Code to deny income tax deductions to employers for contributions to a group health plan unless such plan meets certain continuing coverage requirements.

a. 28-hour day
b. 1990 Clean Air Act
c. 33 Strategies of War
d. Consolidated Omnibus Budget Reconciliation Act

24. A _____ or business method is a collection of related, structured activities or tasks that produce a specific service or product (serve a particular goal) for a particular customer or customers. It often can be visualized with a flowchart as a sequence of activities.

There are three types of _____es:

1. Management processes, the processes that govern the operation of a system. Typical management processes include 'Corporate Governance' and 'Strategic Management'.
2. Operational processes, processes that constitute the core business and create the primary value stream. Typical operational processes are Purchasing, Manufacturing, Marketing, and Sales.
3. Supporting processes, which support the core processes. Examples include Accounting, Recruitment, Technical support.

A _____ begins with a customer's need and ends with a customer's need fulfillment. Process oriented organizations break down the barriers of structural departments and try to avoid functional silos.

a. 33 Strategies of War
b. 28-hour day
c. 1990 Clean Air Act
d. Business process

Chapter 8. Process Measurement and Analysis

1. A _____ is a common type of chart, that represents an algorithm or process, showing the steps as boxes of various kinds, and their order by connecting these with arrows. _____s are used in analyzing, designing, documenting or managing a process or program in various fields.

The first structured method for documenting process flow, the 'flow process chart', was introduced by Frank Gilbreth to members of ASME in 1921 as the presentation 'Process Charts--First Steps in Finding the One Best Way'.

- a. 1990 Clean Air Act
- b. 33 Strategies of War
- c. Flowchart
- d. 28-hour day

2. _____ is the process of comparing the cost, cycle time, productivity, or quality of a specific process or method to another that is widely considered to be an industry standard or best practice. Essentially, _____ provides a snapshot of the performance of your business and helps you understand where you are in relation to a particular standard. The result is often a business case for making changes in order to make improvements.
- a. Cost leadership
- b. Complementors
- c. Competitive heterogeneity
- d. Benchmarking

3. A _____ or business method is a collection of related, structured activities or tasks that produce a specific service or product (serve a particular goal) for a particular customer or customers. It often can be visualized with a flowchart as a sequence of activities.

There are three types of _____es:

1. Management processes, the processes that govern the operation of a system. Typical management processes include 'Corporate Governance' and 'Strategic Management'.
2. Operational processes, processes that constitute the core business and create the primary value stream. Typical operational processes are Purchasing, Manufacturing, Marketing, and Sales.
3. Supporting processes, which support the core processes. Examples include Accounting, Recruitment, Technical support.

A _____ begins with a customer's need and ends with a customer's need fulfillment. Process oriented organizations break down the barriers of structural departments and try to avoid functional silos.

- a. Business process
- b. 33 Strategies of War
- c. 1990 Clean Air Act
- d. 28-hour day

4. _____ refers to metrics and measures of output from production processes, per unit of input. Labor _____, for example, is typically measured as a ratio of output per labor-hour, an input. _____ may be conceived of as a metrics of the technical or engineering efficiency of production.
- a. Productivity
- b. Remanufacturing
- c. Value engineering
- d. Master production schedule

5. _____ is an advertisement in which a particular product specifically mentions a competitor by name for the express purpose of showing why the competitor is inferior to the product naming it.

Chapter 8. Process Measurement and Analysis

This should not be confused with parody advertisements, where a fictional product is being advertised for the purpose of poking fun at the particular advertisement, nor should it be confused with the use of a coined brand name for the purpose of comparing the product without actually naming an actual competitor. ('Wikipedia tastes better and is less filling than the Encyclopedia Galactica.')

In the 1980s, during what has been referred to as the cola wars, soft-drink manufacturer Pepsi ran a series of advertisements where people, caught on hidden camera, in a blind taste test, chose Pepsi over rival Coca-Cola.

- a. 33 Strategies of War
- b. Comparative advertising
- c. 1990 Clean Air Act
- d. 28-hour day

6. In queueing theory, _____ is the proportion of the system's resources which is used by the traffic which arrives at it. It should be strictly less than one for the system to function well. It is usually represented by the symbol ρ.
- a. A Stake in the Outcome
- b. AAAI
- c. Utilization
- d. A4e

7. A _____ is the period of time between the initiation of any process of production and the completion of that process. Thus the _____ for ordering a new car from a manufacturer may be anywhere from 2 weeks to 6 months. In industry, _____ reduction is an important part of lean manufacturing.
- a. 33 Strategies of War
- b. 1990 Clean Air Act
- c. 28-hour day
- d. Lead time

8. _____ is a term applied to an organization that has created the processes, tools, and training to enable it to respond quickly to customer needs and market changes while still controlling costs and quality.

An enabling factor in becoming an agile manufacturer has been the development of manufacturing support technology that allows the marketers, the designers and the production personnel to share a common database of parts and products, to share data on production capacities and problems -- particularly where small initial problems may have larger downstream effects. It is a general proposition of manufacturing that the cost of correcting quality issues increases as the problem moves downstream, so that it is cheaper to correct quality problems at the earliest possible point in the process.

- a. AAAI
- b. A Stake in the Outcome
- c. Agile manufacturing
- d. A4e

9. _____ is defined by APICS as a method for the effective planning of all resources of a manufacturing company. Ideally, it addresses operational planning in units, financial planning in dollars, and has a simulation capability to answer 'what-if' questions and extension of closed-loop _____. Manufacturing resource planning (or Manufacturing resource planning2) - Around 1980, over-frequent changes in sales forecasts, entailing continual readjustments in production, as well as the unsuitability of the parameters fixed by the system, led _____ (Material Requirement Planning) to evolve into a new concept : _____ (e.g. _____ 2)

This is not exclusively a software function, but a marriage of people skills, dedication to data base accuracy, and computer resources.

a. Jidoka
b. Manufacturing resource planning
c. MRP II
d. Homeworkers

10. An _____ is a manufacturing process in which parts (usually interchangeable parts) are added to a product in a sequential manner using optimally planned logistics to create a finished product much faster than with handcrafting-type methods. The _____ developed by Ford Motor Company between 1908 and 1915 made _____ s famous in the following decade through the social ramifications of mass production, such as the affordability of the Ford Model T and the introduction of high wages for Ford workers. However, the various preconditions for the development at Ford stretched far back into the 19th century, from the gradual realization of the dream of interchangeability, to the concept of reinventing workflow and job descriptions using analytical methods.
   a. A Stake in the Outcome
   b. Assembly line
   c. A4e
   d. AAAI

11. _____, a business term, is a measure of how products and services supplied by a company meet or surpass customer expectation. It is seen as a key performance indicator within business and is part of the four perspectives of a Balanced Scorecard.

In a competitive marketplace where businesses compete for customers, _____ is seen as a key differentiator and increasingly has become a key element of business strategy.

   a. Horizontal integration
   b. Critical Success Factor
   c. Foreign ownership
   d. Customer satisfaction

12. _____ is an increasingly broadening term with which an organization, or other human system describes the combination of traditionally administrative personnel functions with acquisition and application of skills, knowledge and experience, Employee Relations and resource planning at various levels. The field draws upon concepts developed in Industrial/Organizational Psychology and System Theory. _____ has at least two related interpretations depending on context. The original usage derives from political economy and economics, where it was traditionally called labor, one of four factors of production although this perspective is changing as a function of new and ongoing research into more strategic approaches at national levels. This first usage is used more in terms of '_____ development', and can go beyond just organizations to the level of nations. The more traditional usage within corporations and businesses refers to the individuals within a firm or agency, and to the portion of the organization that deals with hiring, firing, training, and other personnel issues, typically referred to as `_____ management'.
   a. Human resource management
   b. Human resources
   c. Bradford Factor
   d. Progressive discipline

13. _____ is the use of control systems (such as numerical control, programmable logic control, and other industrial control systems), in concert with other applications of information technology (such as computer-aided technologies [CAD, CAM, CAx]), to control industrial machinery and processes, reducing the need for human intervention. In the scope of industrialization, _____ is a step beyond mechanization. Whereas mechanization provided human operators with machinery to assist them with the physical requirements of work, _____ greatly reduces the need for human sensory and mental requirements as well.
   a. Automation
   b. A4e
   c. A Stake in the Outcome
   d. AAAI

Chapter 8. Process Measurement and Analysis

14. In economics, _____ is the desire to own something and the ability to pay for it. The term _____ signifies the ability or the willingness to buy a particular commodity at a given point of time.
    a. 33 Strategies of War
    b. 28-hour day
    c. 1990 Clean Air Act
    d. Demand

15. _____ is the process of estimation in unknown situations. Prediction is a similar, but more general term. Both can refer to estimation of time series, cross-sectional or longitudinal data.
    a. 28-hour day
    b. 1990 Clean Air Act
    c. 33 Strategies of War
    d. Forecasting

16. _____ is the process whereby an organization establishes the parameters within which programs, investments, and acquisitions are reaching the desired results. Performance Reference Model of the Federal Enterprise Architecture, 2005.

This process of measuring performance often requires the use of statistical evidence to determine progress toward specific defined organizational objectives.

There are many types of measurements.

    a. CIFMS
    b. Crisis management
    c. Performance measurement
    d. Workflow

17. _____ (NYSE: DE) is an American corporation based in Moline, Illinois, and the leading manufacturer of agricultural machinery in the world. In 2008, it was listed as 102nd in the Fortune 500 ranking. Deere and Company agricultural products, usually sold under the John Deere name, include tractors, combine harvesters, balers, planters/seeders, ATVs and forestry equipment.
    a. 1990 Clean Air Act
    b. Deere ' Company
    c. 28-hour day
    d. 33 Strategies of War

18. _____ is, in computer science and management, an approach aiming at improvements by means of elevating efficiency and effectiveness of the business process that exist within and across organizations. The key to _____ is for organizations to look at their business processes from a 'clean slate' perspective and determine how they can best construct these processes to improve how they conduct business. _____ Cycle.

_____ is also known as _____, Business Process Redesign, Business Transformation, or Business Process Change Management.

    a. Horizontal integration
    b. Personal management interview
    c. Product life cycle
    d. Business process reengineering

19. _____ is, in very basic words, a position a firm occupies against its competitors.

According to Michael Porter, the three methods for creating a sustainable _____ are through:

1. Cost leadership

2. Differentiation

3. Focus (economics)

 a. Theory Z
 c. 28-hour day
 b. Competitive advantage
 d. 1990 Clean Air Act

20. _____ is understood as a business unit within the overall corporate identity which is distinguishable from other business because it serves a defined external market where management can conduct strategic planning in relation to products and markets. When companies become really large, they are best thought of as being composed of a number of businesses (or _____s.)

In the broader domain of strategic management, the phrase '_____' came into use in the 1960s, largely as a result of General Electric's many units.

 a. Strategic group
 c. Switching cost
 b. Strategic drift
 d. Strategic business unit

21. In organizational development (OD), _____ is the application of Socio-Technical Systems principles and techniques to the humanization of work.

The aims of _____ to improved job satisfaction, to improved through-put, to improved quality and to reduced employee problems, e.g., grievances, absenteeism.

Under scientific management people would be directed by reason and the problems of industrial unrest would be appropriately (i.e., scientifically) addressed.

 a. Path-goal theory
 c. Work design
 b. Management process
 d. Graduate recruitment

22. _____ is a theory of management that analyzes and synthesizes workflows, with the objective of improving labour productivity. The core ideas of the theory were developed by Frederick Winslow Taylor in the 1880s and 1890s, and were first published in his monographs, Shop Management and The Principles of _____ Taylor believed that decisions based upon tradition and rules of thumb should be replaced by precise procedures developed after careful study of an individual at work.

 a. Value engineering
 c. Capacity planning
 b. Master production schedule
 d. Scientific management

23. _____ is a business management strategy, initially implemented by Motorola, that today enjoys widespread application in many sectors of industry.

Chapter 8. Process Measurement and Analysis

_____ seeks to improve the quality of process outputs by identifying and removing the causes of defects (errors) and variation in manufacturing and business processes. It uses a set of quality management methods, including statistical methods, and creates a special infrastructure of people within the organization ('Black Belts' etc.)

a. Six sigma
b. Theory of constraints
c. Takt time
d. Production line

24. _____ refers to training in different ways to improve overall performance. It takes advantage of the particular effectiveness of each training method, while at the same time attempting to neglect the shortcomings of that method by combining it with other methods that address its weaknesses.

Cross training is employee-employer field means, training employees to do one another's work.

a. 33 Strategies of War
b. 28-hour day
c. 1990 Clean Air Act
d. Cross-training

25. A _____ is an entity formed between two or more parties to undertake economic activity together. The parties agree to create a new entity by both contributing equity, and they then share in the revenues, expenses, and control of the enterprise. The venture can be for one specific project only, or a continuing business relationship such as the Fuji Xerox _____.

a. Joint venture
b. Civil Rights Act of 1991
c. Meritor Savings Bank v. Vinson
d. Patent

26. _____ can be considered to have three main components: quality control, quality assurance and quality improvement. _____ is focused not only on product quality, but also the means to achieve it. _____ therefore uses quality assurance and control of processes as well as products to achieve more consistent quality.

a. Quality management
b. 28-hour day
c. Total quality management
d. 1990 Clean Air Act

27. _____ is a business management strategy aimed at embedding awareness of quality in all organizational processes. _____ has been widely used in manufacturing, education, hospitals, call centers, government, and service industries, as well as NASA space and science programs.

As defined by the International Organization for Standardization (ISO):

'_____ is a management approach for an organization, centered on quality, based on the participation of all its members and aiming at long-term success through customer satisfaction, and benefits to all members of the organization and to society.' ISO 8402:1994

One major aim is to reduce variation from every process so that greater consistency of effort is obtained. (Royse, D., Thyer, B., Padgett D., ' Logan T., 2006)

Chapter 8. Process Measurement and Analysis

a. Total quality management
b. 1990 Clean Air Act
c. 28-hour day
d. Quality management

28. An _____ is a person who has possession of an enterprise and assumes significant accountability for the inherent risks and the outcome. It is an ambitious leader who combines land, labor, and capital to create and market new goods or services. The term is a loanword from French and was first defined by the Irish economist Richard Cantillon.
   a. A4e
   b. AAAI
   c. A Stake in the Outcome
   d. Entrepreneur

29. _____ refers to increasing the spiritual, political, social or economic strength of individuals and communities. It often involves the empowered developing confidence in their own capacities.

The term Human _____ covers a vast landscape of meanings, interpretations, definitions and disciplines ranging from psychology and philosophy to the highly commercialized Self-Help industry and Motivational sciences.

   a. AAAI
   b. A4e
   c. A Stake in the Outcome
   d. Empowerment

30. The term '_____' refers to the concept of collecting information and attempting to spot a pattern in the information. In some fields of study, the term '_____' has more formally-defined meanings.

In project management _____ is a mathematical technique that uses historical results to predict future outcome.

   a. Regression analysis
   b. Stepwise regression
   c. Trend analysis
   d. Least squares

31. _____, e-commuting, e-work, telework, working from home (WFH), or working at home (WAH) is a work arrangement in which employees enjoy flexibility in working location and hours. In other words, the daily commute to a central place of work is replaced by telecommunication links. Many work from home, while others, occasionally also referred to as nomad workers or web commuters utilize mobile telecommunications technology to work from coffee shops or myriad other locations.
   a. 33 Strategies of War
   b. 28-hour day
   c. 1990 Clean Air Act
   d. Telecommuting

32. _____ means increasing the scope of a job through extending the range of its job duties and responsibilities. This contradicts the principles of specialisation and the division of labour whereby work is divided into small units, each of which is performed repetitively by an individual worker. Some motivational theories suggest that the boredom and alienation caused by the division of labour can actually cause efficiency to fall.
   a. Job enlargement
   b. Mock interview
   c. Centralization
   d. Delayering

33. _____ is an attempt to motivate employees by giving them the opportunity to use the range of their abilities. It is an idea that was developed by the American psychologist Frederick Herzberg in the 1950s. It can be contrasted to job enlargement which simply increases the number of tasks without changing the challenge.

a. Cash cow
b. Catfish effect
c. C-A-K-E
d. Job enrichment

34. A _____ is a computer program typically used to provide some form of artificial intelligence, which consists primarily of a set of rules about behavior. These rules, termed productions, are a basic representation found useful in AI planning, expert systems and action selection. A _____ provides the mechanism necessary to execute productions in order to achieve some goal for the system.
   a. 33 Strategies of War
   b. 28-hour day
   c. 1990 Clean Air Act
   d. Production system

35. The metastability in flip-flops can be avoided by ensuring that the data and control inputs are held valid and constant for specified periods before and after the clock pulse, called the _____ and the hold time (t_h) respectively. These times are specified in the data sheet for the device, and are typically between a few nanoseconds and a few hundred picoseconds for modern devices.

Unfortunately, it is not always possible to meet the setup and hold criteria, because the flip-flop may be connected to a real-time signal that could change at any time, outside the control of the designer.

   a. 33 Strategies of War
   b. 28-hour day
   c. 1990 Clean Air Act
   d. Setup time

36. _____ is also known as operations management, management science, systems engineering, or manufacturing engineering; a distinction that seems to depend on the viewpoint or motives of the user. Recruiters or educational establishments use the names to differentiate themselves from others. In healthcare, for example, industrial engineers are more commonly known as management engineers or health systems engineers.
   a. AAAI
   b. Industrial engineering
   c. A Stake in the Outcome
   d. A4e

37. The International Brotherhood of _____ is a labor union in the United States and Canada. Formed in 1903 by the merger of several local and regional locals of _____, the union now represents a diverse membership of blue-collar and professional workers in both the public and private sectors. The union had approximately 1.4 million members in 2007.
   a. 33 Strategies of War
   b. 1990 Clean Air Act
   c. 28-hour day
   d. Teamsters

Chapter 9. Quality Management

1. _____ is the provision of service to customers before, during and after a purchase.

According to Turban et al. (2002), '_____ is a series of activities designed to enhance the level of customer satisfaction - that is, the feeling that a product or service has met the customer expectation.'

Its importance varies by product, industry and customer; defective or broken merchandise can be exchanged, often only with a receipt and within a specified time frame.

   a. 1990 Clean Air Act
   b. 28-hour day
   c. Service rate
   d. Customer service

2. _____ is an advertisement in which a particular product specifically mentions a competitor by name for the express purpose of showing why the competitor is inferior to the product naming it.

This should not be confused with parody advertisements, where a fictional product is being advertised for the purpose of poking fun at the particular advertisement, nor should it be confused with the use of a coined brand name for the purpose of comparing the product without actually naming an actual competitor. ('Wikipedia tastes better and is less filling than the Encyclopedia Galactica.')

In the 1980s, during what has been referred to as the cola wars, soft-drink manufacturer Pepsi ran a series of advertisements where people, caught on hidden camera, in a blind taste test, chose Pepsi over rival Coca-Cola.

   a. 33 Strategies of War
   b. Comparative advertising
   c. 1990 Clean Air Act
   d. 28-hour day

3. _____ ('Plan-Do-Check-Act') is an iterative four-step problem-solving process typically used in business process improvement. It is also known as the Deming Cycle, Shewhart cycle, Deming Wheel, or Plan-Do-Study-Act.

_____ was made popular by Dr. W. Edwards Deming, who is considered by many to be the father of modern quality control; however it was always referred to by him as the Shewhart cycle. Later in Deming's career, he modified _____ to Plan, Do, Study, Act (PDSA) so as to better describe his recommendations.

   a. Management team
   b. Management by exception
   c. Decentralization
   d. PDCA

4. In economics, business, retail, and accounting, a _____ is the value of money that has been used up to produce something, and hence is not available for use anymore. In economics, a _____ is an alternative that is given up as a result of a decision. In business, the _____ may be one of acquisition, in which case the amount of money expended to acquire it is counted as _____.
   a. Cost overrun
   b. Fixed costs
   c. Cost
   d. Cost allocation

Chapter 9. Quality Management

5. The _____ is given by the United States National Institute of Standards and Technology. Through the actions of the National Productivity Advisory Committee chaired by Jack Grayson, it was established by the Malcolm Baldrige National Quality Improvement Act of 1987 - Public Law 100-107 and named for Malcolm Baldrige, who served as United States Secretary of Commerce during the Reagan administration from 1981 until his 1987 death in a rodeo accident. APQC, , organized the first White House Conference on Productivity, spearheading the creation and design of the _____ in 1987, and jointly administering the award for its first three years.

    a. Malcolm Baldrige National Quality Award   b. Time and attendance
    c. Business Network Transformation   d. Scenario planning

6. _____ is a costing model that identifies activities in an organization and assigns the cost of each activity resource to all products and services according to the actual consumption by each: it assigns more indirect costs (overhead) into direct costs.

In this way an organization can establish the true cost of its individual products and services for the purposes of identifying and eliminating those which are unprofitable and lowering the prices of those which are overpriced.

In a business organization, the ABC methodology assigns an organization's resource costs through activities to the products and services provided to its customers.

    a. A Stake in the Outcome   b. Indirect costs
    c. A4e   d. Activity-based costing

7. The concept of _____ is a means to quantify the total cost of quality-related efforts and deficiencies. It was first described by Armand V. Feigenbaum in a 1956 Harvard Business Review article.

Prior to its introduction, the general perception was that higher quality requires higher costs, either by buying better materials or machines or by hiring more labor.

    a. Quality Costs   b. Variable cost
    c. Cost overrun   d. Transaction cost

8. _____ is the process whereby an organization establishes the parameters within which programs, investments, and acquisitions are reaching the desired results. Performance Reference Model of the Federal Enterprise Architecture, 2005.

This process of measuring performance often requires the use of statistical evidence to determine progress toward specific defined organizational objectives.

There are many types of measurements.

    a. Crisis management   b. CIFMS
    c. Workflow   d. Performance measurement

Chapter 9. Quality Management

9. In engineering and manufacturing, _____ and quality engineering are used in developing systems to ensure products or services are designed and produced to meet or exceed customer requirements. Refer to the definition by Merriam-Webster for further information . These systems are often developed in conjunction with other business and engineering disciplines using a cross-functional approach.
   a. Single Minute Exchange of Die
   b. Process capability
   c. Statistical process control
   d. Quality control

10. _____ is one of the managerial functions like planning, organizing, staffing and directing. It is an important function because it helps to check the errors and to take the corrective action so that deviation from standards are minimized and stated goals of the organization are achieved in desired manner.According to modern concepts, _____ is a foreseeing action whereas earlier concept of _____ was used only when errors were detected. _____ in management means setting standards, measuring actual performance and taking corrective action.
   a. Schedule of reinforcement
   b. Turnover
   c. Decision tree pruning
   d. Control

11. _____ is the process of estimation in unknown situations. Prediction is a similar, but more general term. Both can refer to estimation of time series, cross-sectional or longitudinal data.
   a. 33 Strategies of War
   b. 1990 Clean Air Act
   c. 28-hour day
   d. Forecasting

12. In organizational development (OD), _____ is the application of Socio-Technical Systems principles and techniques to the humanization of work.

The aims of _____ to improved job satisfaction, to improved through-put, to improved quality and to reduced employee problems, e.g., grievances, absenteeism.

Under scientific management people would be directed by reason and the problems of industrial unrest would be appropriately (i.e., scientifically) addressed.

   a. Graduate recruitment
   b. Management process
   c. Path-goal theory
   d. Work design

13. _____ refers to training in different ways to improve overall performance. It takes advantage of the particular effectiveness of each training method, while at the same time attempting to neglect the shortcomings of that method by combining it with other methods that address its weaknesses.

Cross training is employee-employer field means, training employees to do one another's work.

   a. Cross-training
   b. 28-hour day
   c. 33 Strategies of War
   d. 1990 Clean Air Act

14. A _____ or business method is a collection of related, structured activities or tasks that produce a specific service or product (serve a particular goal) for a particular customer or customers. It often can be visualized with a flowchart as a sequence of activities.

There are three types of _____ es:

1. Management processes, the processes that govern the operation of a system. Typical management processes include 'Corporate Governance' and 'Strategic Management'.
2. Operational processes, processes that constitute the core business and create the primary value stream. Typical operational processes are Purchasing, Manufacturing, Marketing, and Sales.
3. Supporting processes, which support the core processes. Examples include Accounting, Recruitment, Technical support.

A _____ begins with a customer's need and ends with a customer's need fulfillment. Process oriented organizations break down the barriers of structural departments and try to avoid functional silos.

a. 33 Strategies of War
b. 28-hour day
c. 1990 Clean Air Act
d. Business process

15. The act of becoming a surety is also called a _____. Traditionally a _____ was distinguished from a surety in that the surety's liability was joint and primary with the principal, whereas the guaranty's liability was ancillary and derivative, but many jurisdictions have abolished this distinction
a. Blue sky law
b. National treatment
c. Clayton Antitrust Act
d. Guarantee

16. An _____ is a manufacturing process in which parts (usually interchangeable parts) are added to a product in a sequential manner using optimally planned logistics to create a finished product much faster than with handcrafting-type methods. The _____ developed by Ford Motor Company between 1908 and 1915 made _____s famous in the following decade through the social ramifications of mass production, such as the affordability of the Ford Model T and the introduction of high wages for Ford workers. However, the various preconditions for the development at Ford stretched far back into the 19th century, from the gradual realization of the dream of interchangeability, to the concept of reinventing workflow and job descriptions using analytical methods.
a. Assembly line
b. A4e
c. A Stake in the Outcome
d. AAAI

17. In probability theory, a probability distribution is called _____ if its cumulative distribution function is _____. This is equivalent to saying that for random variables X with the distribution in question, $Pr[X = a] = 0$ for all real numbers a, i.e.: the probability that X attains the value a is zero, for any number a. If the distribution of X is _____ then X is called a _____ random variable.
a. Pay Band
b. Connectionist expert systems
c. Decision tree pruning
d. Continuous

18. _____ is a management process whereby delivery (customer valued) processes are constantly evaluated and improved in the light of their efficiency, effectiveness and flexibility.

Some see it as a meta process for most management systems (Business Process Management, Quality Management, Project Management). Deming saw it as part of the 'system' whereby feedback from the process and customer were evaluated against organisational goals.

Chapter 9. Quality Management

a. Critical Success Factor
b. Continuous Improvement Process
c. Sole proprietorship
d. First-mover advantage

19. _____ is a Japanese philosophy that focuses on continuous improvement throughout all aspects of life. When applied to the workplace, _____ activities continually improve all functions of a business, from manufacturing to management and from the CEO to the assembly line workers. By improving standardized activities and processes, _____ aims to eliminate waste .

a. Kaizen
b. Cross-docking
c. Psychological pricing
d. Sensitivity analysis

20. _____ or lean production, which is often known simply as 'Lean', is a production practice that considers the expenditure of resources for any goal other than the creation of value for the end customer to be wasteful, and thus a target for elimination. Working from the perspective of the customer who consumes a product or service, 'value' is defined as any action or process that a customer would be willing to pay for. Basically, lean is centered around creating more value with less work.

a. Theory of constraints
b. Production line
c. Six Sigma
d. Lean manufacturing

21. _____ is a Japanese term that means 'fail-safing' or 'mistake-proofing'. A _____ is any mechanism in a Lean manufacturing process that helps an equipment operator avoid (yokeru) mistakes (poka.) Its purpose is to eliminate product defects by preventing, correcting, or drawing attention to human errors as they occur.

a. 28-hour day
b. 1990 Clean Air Act
c. 33 Strategies of War
d. Poka-yoke

22. _____ is a business management strategy aimed at embedding awareness of quality in all organizational processes. _____ has been widely used in manufacturing, education, hospitals, call centers, government, and service industries, as well as NASA space and science programs.

As defined by the International Organization for Standardization (ISO):

'_____ is a management approach for an organization, centered on quality, based on the participation of all its members and aiming at long-term success through customer satisfaction, and benefits to all members of the organization and to society.' ISO 8402:1994

One major aim is to reduce variation from every process so that greater consistency of effort is obtained. (Royse, D., Thyer, B., Padgett D., ' Logan T., 2006)

a. Quality management
b. Total quality management
c. 28-hour day
d. 1990 Clean Air Act

23. _____ can be considered to have three main components: quality control, quality assurance and quality improvement. _____ is focused not only on product quality, but also the means to achieve it. _____ therefore uses quality assurance and control of processes as well as products to achieve more consistent quality.

a. 28-hour day
b. Total quality management
c. Quality management
d. 1990 Clean Air Act

Chapter 9. Quality Management

24. _____ is a business management strategy, initially implemented by Motorola, that today enjoys widespread application in many sectors of industry.

_____ seeks to improve the quality of process outputs by identifying and removing the causes of defects (errors) and variation in manufacturing and business processes. It uses a set of quality management methods, including statistical methods, and creates a special infrastructure of people within the organization ('Black Belts' etc.)

a. Six sigma
b. Theory of constraints
c. Production line
d. Takt time

25. _____ is the process of comparing the cost, cycle time, productivity, or quality of a specific process or method to another that is widely considered to be an industry standard or best practice. Essentially, _____ provides a snapshot of the performance of your business and helps you understand where you are in relation to a particular standard. The result is often a business case for making changes in order to make improvements.

a. Competitive heterogeneity
b. Cost leadership
c. Complementors
d. Benchmarking

26. _____ is an area of business concerned with the production of goods and services, and involves the responsibility of ensuring that business operations are efficient in terms of using as little resource as needed, and effective in terms of meeting customer requirements. It is concerned with managing the process that converts inputs (in the forms of materials, labour and energy) into outputs (in the form of goods and services.)

Operations traditionally refers to the production of goods and services separately, although the distinction between these two main types of operations is increasingly difficult to make as manufacturers tend to merge product and service offerings.

a. A4e
b. AAAI
c. A Stake in the Outcome
d. Operations Management

27. _____ is subcontracting a process, such as product design or manufacturing, to a third-party company. The decision to outsource is often made in the interest of lowering cost or making better use of time and energy costs, redirecting or conserving energy directed at the competencies of a particular business, or to make more efficient use of land, labor, capital, (information) technology and resources. _____ became part of the business lexicon during the 1980s.

a. Unemployment insurance
b. Operant conditioning
c. Outsourcing
d. Opinion leadership

28. _____, a business term, is a measure of how products and services supplied by a company meet or surpass customer expectation. It is seen as a key performance indicator within business and is part of the four perspectives of a Balanced Scorecard.

In a competitive marketplace where businesses compete for customers, _____ is seen as a key differentiator and increasingly has become a key element of business strategy.

Chapter 9. Quality Management 73

a. Horizontal integration
c. Foreign ownership
b. Critical Success Factor
d. Customer satisfaction

29. _____ is an inventory strategy that strives to improve the return on investment of a business by reducing in-process inventory and its associated carrying costs. To meet _____ objectives, the process relies on signals between different points in the process. This means the process is often driven by a series of signals, or Kanban , which tell production when to make the next part. Kanban are usually 'tickets' but can be simple visual signals, such as the presence or absence of a part on a shelf. Implemented correctly, _____ can dramatically improve a manufacturing organization's return on investment, quality, and efficiency.
 a. 28-hour day
 c. 33 Strategies of War
 b. 1990 Clean Air Act
 d. Just-in-time

30. The _____, widely known as ISO , is an international-standard-setting body composed of representatives from various national standards organizations. Founded on 23 February 1947, the organization promulgates worldwide proprietary industrial and commercial standards. It is headquartered in Geneva, Switzerland.
 a. A4e
 c. AAAI
 b. International Organization for Standardization
 d. A Stake in the Outcome

31. The general definition of an _____ is an evaluation of a person, organization, system, process, project or product. _____s are performed to ascertain the validity and reliability of information; also to provide an assessment of a system's internal control. The goal of an _____ is to express an opinion on the person / organization/system (etc) in question, under evaluation based on work done on a test basis.
 a. Internal control
 c. Audit
 b. A Stake in the Outcome
 d. Audit committee

32. _____ is a broad label that refers to any individuals or households that use goods and services generated within the economy. The concept of a _____ is used in different contexts, so that the usage and significance of the term may vary.

Typically when business people and economists talk of _____s they are talking about person as _____, an aggregated commodity item with little individuality other than that expressed in the buy/not-buy decision.

 a. 1990 Clean Air Act
 c. 33 Strategies of War
 b. Consumer
 d. 28-hour day

33. The International Brotherhood of _____ is a labor union in the United States and Canada. Formed in 1903 by the merger of several local and regional locals of _____, the union now represents a diverse membership of blue-collar and professional workers in both the public and private sectors. The union had approximately 1.4 million members in 2007.
 a. 33 Strategies of War
 c. 1990 Clean Air Act
 b. 28-hour day
 d. Teamsters

34. A _____ is a common type of chart, that represents an algorithm or process, showing the steps as boxes of various kinds, and their order by connecting these with arrows. _____s are used in analyzing, designing, documenting or managing a process or program in various fields.

Chapter 9. Quality Management

The first structured method for documenting process flow, the 'flow process chart', was introduced by Frank Gilbreth to members of ASME in 1921 as the presentation 'Process Charts--First Steps in Finding the One Best Way'.

a. 28-hour day
b. 1990 Clean Air Act
c. 33 Strategies of War
d. Flowchart

35. In statistics, a _____ is a graphical display of tabulated frequencies, shown as bars. It shows what proportion of cases fall into each of several categories: it is a form of data binning. The categories are usually specified as non-overlapping intervals of some variable.

a. Correlation
b. Statistics
c. Standard deviation
d. Histogram

36. A _____ is a special type of bar chart where the values being plotted are arranged in descending order. The graph is accompanied by a line graph which shows the cumulative totals of each category, left to right. The chart was named for Vilfredo Pareto.

a. 1990 Clean Air Act
b. 33 Strategies of War
c. Pareto chart
d. 28-hour day

37. A _____ is a type of display using Cartesian coordinates to display values for two variables for a set of data.

The data is displayed as a collection of points, each having the value of one variable determining the position on the horizontal axis and the value of the other variable determining the position on the vertical axis. A _____ is also called a scatter chart, scatter diagram and scatter graph.

a. 28-hour day
b. 33 Strategies of War
c. 1990 Clean Air Act
d. Scatter plot

38. The _____ is a business tool used to organize ideas and data. It is one of the Seven Management and Planning Tools.

The tool is commonly used within project management and allows large numbers of ideas to be sorted into groups for review and analysis.

The _____ was devised by Jiro Kawakita in the 1960s and is sometimes referred to as the KJ Method.

a. A4e
b. Affinity diagram
c. AAAI
d. A Stake in the Outcome

39. A _____ is a decision support tool that uses a tree-like graph or model of decisions and their possible consequences, including chance event outcomes, resource costs, and utility. _____s are commonly used in operations research, specifically in decision analysis, to help identify a strategy most likely to reach a goal. Another use of _____s is as a descriptive means for calculating conditional probabilities.

Chapter 9. Quality Management

a. 1990 Clean Air Act
b. 28-hour day
c. Decision tree
d. 33 Strategies of War

40. In decision theory and estimation theory, the _____ of an estimator, $\hat{\theta}$, of an unknown parameter of the distribution, θ, is the expected value of the loss function

$$R(\theta, \hat{\theta}) = \mathbb{E}_\theta L(\theta, \hat{\theta}) = \int L(\theta, \hat{\theta})\, dP_\theta.$$

where dP_θ is a probability measure parametrized by θ.

- For a scalar parameter θ and a quadratic loss function,

$$L(\theta, \hat{\theta}) = (\theta - \hat{\theta})^2$$

  the _____ function becomes the mean squared error of the estimate,

$$R(\theta, \hat{\theta}) = E_\theta (\theta - \hat{\theta})^2$$

- In density estimation, the unknown parameter is probability density itself. The loss function is typically chosen to be a norm in an appropriate function space. For example, for L^2 norm,

$$L(f, \hat{f}) = \|f - \hat{f}\|_2^2$$

  the _____ function becomes the mean integrated squared error

$$R(f, \hat{f}) = E\|f - \hat{f}\|^2$$

a. Risk
b. Linear model
c. Financial modeling
d. Risk aversion

Chapter 9. Quality Management

41. In quality assessment, _____ is an inspection standard describing the maximum number of defects that could be considered acceptable during the random sampling of an inspection. The defects found during inspection are classified into three levels: critical, major and minor. Broadly, these levels are defined as follows:

- Critical defects are those that render the product unsafe or hazardous for the end user, or that contravene mandatory regulations.

- Major defects can result in the product's failure, reducing its marketability, usability, or saleability.

- Minor defects do not affect the product's marketability or usability, but represent workmanship defects that make the product fall short of defined quality standards.

Different companies maintain different interpretations of each defect type.

a. AAAI
b. A4e
c. A Stake in the Outcome
d. Acceptable quality level

42. The _____ Automobile Company is an automobile manufacturer based in Wolfsburg, Germany, and is the original brand within the _____ Group, as well as the largest brand by sales volume.

_____ means 'people's car' in German, in which it is pronounced . Its current tagline or slogan is Das Auto .

a. Competence-based Strategic Management
b. Volkswagen
c. Rate of return
d. Turnover

43. In differential topology, a _____ of a differentiable function between differentiable manifolds is the image of a critical point.

The basic result on _____s is Sard's lemma. The set of _____s can be quite irregular; but in Morse theory it becomes important to consider real-valued functions on a manifold M, such that the set of _____s is in fact finite.

a. Critical value
b. 28-hour day
c. 33 Strategies of War
d. 1990 Clean Air Act

44. _____ is an effective method of monitoring a process through the use of control charts. Control charts enable the use of objective criteria for distinguishing background variation from events of significance based on statistical techniques. Much of its power lies in the ability to monitor both process center and its variation about that center.

a. Process capability
b. Single Minute Exchange of Die
c. Quality control
d. Statistical process control

45. In probability theory, the _____ states conditions under which the sum of a sufficiently large number of independent random variables, each with finite mean and variance, will be approximately normally distributed . Since real-world quantities are often the balanced sum of many unobserved random events, this theorem provides a partial explanation for the prevalence of the normal probability distribution. The _____ also justifies the approximation of large-sample statistics to the normal distribution in controlled experiments.

Chapter 9. Quality Management

a. Central limit theorem
b. Point biserial correlation coefficient
c. Heavy-tailed distributions
d. Pay Band

46. In probability theory and statistics, the _____ or Gaussian distribution is a continuous probability distribution that describes data that clusters around a mean or average. The graph of the associated probability density function is bell-shaped, with a peak at the mean, and is known as the Gaussian function or bell curve.

The _____ can be used to describe, at least approximately, any variable that tends to cluster around the mean.

a. Histogram
b. Normal distribution
c. Heteroskedastic
d. Generalized normal distribution

47. _____ is one of the four elements of marketing mix. An organization or set of organizations (go-betweens) involved in the process of making a product or service available for use or consumption by a consumer or business user.

The other three parts of the marketing mix are product, pricing, and promotion.

a. Matching theory
b. Job creation programs
c. Missing completely at random
d. Distribution

48. The _____ is a measurable property of a process to the specification, expressed as a _____ index (e.g., C_{pk} or C_{pm}) or as a process performance index (e.g., P_{pk} or P_{pm}.) The output of this measurement is usually illustrated by a histogram and calculations that predict how many parts will be produced out of specification.

_____ is also defined as the capability of a process to meet its purpose as managed by an organization's management and process definition structures ISO 15504.

a. Process capability
b. Quality control
c. Single Minute Exchange of Die
d. Statistical process control

49. The _____ in statistical process control is a tool used to determine whether a manufacturing or business process is in a state of statistical control or not.

If the chart indicates that the process is currently under control then it can be used with confidence to predict the future performance of the process. If the chart indicates that the process being monitored is not in control, the pattern it reveals can help determine the source of variation to be eliminated to bring the process back into control.

a. Simple moving average
b. Control chart
c. Time series analysis
d. Failure rate

50. In process improvement efforts, the process capability index or _____ is a statistical measure of process capability: The ability of a process to produce output within engineering tolerances and specification limits. The concept of process capability only holds meaning for processes that are in a state of statistical control.

If the upper and lower specifications of the process are USL and LSL, the target process mean is T, the estimated mean of the process is $\hat{\mu}$ and the estimated variability of the process (expressed as a standard deviation) is $\hat{\sigma}$, then commonly-accepted process capability indices include:

$\hat{\sigma}$ is estimated using the sample standard deviation.

- a. Process capability ratio
- b. 1990 Clean Air Act
- c. Constant dollars
- d. Process capability index

51. _____ are horizontal lines drawn on an statistical process control chart, usually at a distance of >±3 standard deviations of the plotted statistic from the statistic's mean.

For normally distributed statistics, the area bracketed by the _____ will on average contain 99.73% of all the plot points on the chart, as long as the process is and remains in statistical control.

_____ should not be confused with tolerance limits, which are completely independent of the distribution of the plotted sample statistic.

- a. Skewness risk
- b. 1990 Clean Air Act
- c. Control limits
- d. T-statistic

52. An _____ is a specific member of a family of control charts. A control chart is a tool used in quality control, specifically SPC or statistical process control, as originally developed by Walter A. Shewhart at Western Electric in 1924 to improve the quality of telephones.

A control chart is a plot of measurements of a product on two special scales, usually located above and below each other and running horizontally. _____s consist of two charts, both with the same horizontal axis denoting the sample number.

- a. X-bar/R chart
- b. 1990 Clean Air Act
- c. 33 Strategies of War
- d. 28-hour day

53. _____ are statistical methods developed by Genichi Taguchi to improve the quality of manufactured goods, and more recently also applied to biotechnology, marketing and advertising. Professional statisticians have welcomed the goals and improvements brought about by _____, particularly by Taguchi's development of designs for studying variation, but have criticized the inefficiency of some of Taguchi's proposals.

Taguchi's work includes three principal contributions to statistics:

1. Taguchi loss function;
2. The philosophy of off-line quality control; and
3. Innovations in the design of experiments.

Chapter 9. Quality Management

Traditionally, statistical methods have relied on mean-unbiased estimators of treatment effects: Under the conditions of the Gauss-Markov theorem, least squares estimators have minimum variance among all mean-unbiased estimators. The emphasis on comparisons of means also draws (limiting) comfort from the law of large numbers, according to which the sample means converge to the true mean.

a. 1990 Clean Air Act
b. Design of experiments
c. 28-hour day
d. Taguchi methods

54. In business and engineering, _____ is the term used to describe the complete process of bringing a new product or service to market. There are two parallel paths involved in the _____ process: one involves the idea generation, product design, and detail engineering; the other involves market research and marketing analysis. Companies typically see _____ as the first stage in generating and commercializing new products within the overall strategic process of product life cycle management used to maintain or grow their market share.

a. 33 Strategies of War
b. 1990 Clean Air Act
c. New product development
d. 28-hour day

55. In statistics, decision theory and economics, a _____ is a function that maps an event (technically an element of a sample space) onto a real number representing the economic cost or regret associated with the event.

Less technically, in statistics a _____ represents the loss (cost in money or loss in utility in some other sense) associated with an estimate being 'wrong' (different from either a desired or a true value) as a function of a measure of the degree of wrongness (generally the difference between the estimated value and the true or desired value.)

Both Frequentist and Bayesian statistical theory involve calculating statistics in such a way as to minimize the expected loss observed from being wrong given a set of assumptions about the data and one's _____.

a. 28-hour day
b. 1990 Clean Air Act
c. 33 Strategies of War
d. Loss function

56. In business and engineering, new _____ is the term used to describe the complete process of bringing a new product or service to market. There are two parallel paths involved in the NProduct development process: one involves the idea generation, product design, and detail engineering; the other involves market research and marketing analysis. Companies typically see new _____ as the first stage in generating and commercializing new products within the overall strategic process of product life cycle management used to maintain or grow their market share.

a. 33 Strategies of War
b. 1990 Clean Air Act
c. Product development
d. 28-hour day

Chapter 10. Lean Production

1. A _____ is a computer program typically used to provide some form of artificial intelligence, which consists primarily of a set of rules about behavior. These rules, termed productions, are a basic representation found useful in AI planning, expert systems and action selection. A _____ provides the mechanism necessary to execute productions in order to achieve some goal for the system.
   a. 33 Strategies of War
   b. 28-hour day
   c. Production System
   d. 1990 Clean Air Act

2. _____ is a theory of management that analyzes and synthesizes workflows, with the objective of improving labour productivity. The core ideas of the theory were developed by Frederick Winslow Taylor in the 1880s and 1890s, and were first published in his monographs, Shop Management and The Principles of _____. Taylor believed that decisions based upon tradition and rules of thumb should be replaced by precise procedures developed after careful study of an individual at work.
   a. Value engineering
   b. Capacity planning
   c. Master production schedule
   d. Scientific management

3. An _____ is a manufacturing process in which parts (usually interchangeable parts) are added to a product in a sequential manner using optimally planned logistics to create a finished product much faster than with handcrafting-type methods. The _____ developed by Ford Motor Company between 1908 and 1915 made _____s famous in the following decade through the social ramifications of mass production, such as the affordability of the Ford Model T and the introduction of high wages for Ford workers. However, the various preconditions for the development at Ford stretched far back into the 19th century, from the gradual realization of the dream of interchangeability, to the concept of reinventing workflow and job descriptions using analytical methods.
   a. AAAI
   b. Assembly line
   c. A Stake in the Outcome
   d. A4e

4. In economics, _____s are key economic variables that economists used to predict a new phase of the business cycle. A _____ is one that changes before the economy does; a lagging indicator is one that changes after the economy has changed. Examples of _____s include stock prices, which often improve or worsen before a similar change in the economy.
   a. Deflation
   b. Human capital
   c. Perfect competition
   d. Leading indicator

5. _____ is the process of comparing the cost, cycle time, productivity, or quality of a specific process or method to another that is widely considered to be an industry standard or best practice. Essentially, _____ provides a snapshot of the performance of your business and helps you understand where you are in relation to a particular standard. The result is often a business case for making changes in order to make improvements.
   a. Cost leadership
   b. Competitive heterogeneity
   c. Complementors
   d. Benchmarking

6. Autonomation describes a feature of machine design to effect the principle of _____ used in the Toyota Production System (TPS) and Lean manufacturing. It may be described as 'intelligent automation' or 'automation with a human touch.' This type of automation implements some supervisory functions rather than production functions. At Toyota this usually means that if an abnormal situation arises the machine stops and the worker will stop the production line.
   a. Manufacturing resource planning
   b. MRP II
   c. Homeworkers
   d. Jidoka

Chapter 10. Lean Production

7. _____ describes a feature of machine design to effect the principle of jidoka (è‡ªåƒ åŒ–) used in the Toyota Production System (TPS) and Lean manufacturing. It may be described as 'intelligent automation' or 'automation with a human touch.' This type of automation implements some supervisory functions rather than production functions. At Toyota this usually means that if an abnormal situation arises the machine stops and the worker will stop the production line.
- a. A4e
- b. AAAI
- c. A Stake in the Outcome
- d. Autonomation

8. _____ is an inventory strategy that strives to improve the return on investment of a business by reducing in-process inventory and its associated carrying costs. To meet _____ objectives, the process relies on signals between different points in the process. This means the process is often driven by a series of signals, or Kanban, which tell production when to make the next part. Kanban are usually 'tickets' but can be simple visual signals, such as the presence or absence of a part on a shelf. Implemented correctly, _____ can dramatically improve a manufacturing organization's return on investment, quality, and efficiency.
- a. 28-hour day
- b. 1990 Clean Air Act
- c. 33 Strategies of War
- d. Just-in-time

9. _____ or lean production, which is often known simply as 'Lean', is a production practice that considers the expenditure of resources for any goal other than the creation of value for the end customer to be wasteful, and thus a target for elimination. Working from the perspective of the customer who consumes a product or service, 'value' is defined as any action or process that a customer would be willing to pay for. Basically, lean is centered around creating more value with less work.
- a. Lean manufacturing
- b. Theory of constraints
- c. Production line
- d. Six Sigma

10. _____, a business term, is a measure of how products and services supplied by a company meet or surpass customer expectation. It is seen as a key performance indicator within business and is part of the four perspectives of a Balanced Scorecard.

In a competitive marketplace where businesses compete for customers, _____ is seen as a key differentiator and increasingly has become a key element of business strategy.

- a. Foreign ownership
- b. Critical Success Factor
- c. Horizontal integration
- d. Customer satisfaction

11. _____ is the process of estimation in unknown situations. Prediction is a similar, but more general term. Both can refer to estimation of time series, cross-sectional or longitudinal data.
- a. 1990 Clean Air Act
- b. 28-hour day
- c. Forecasting
- d. 33 Strategies of War

12. _____ is the management of the flow of goods, information and other resources, including energy and people, between the point of origin and the point of consumption in order to meet the requirements of consumers (frequently, and originally, military organizations.) _____ involves the integration of information, transportation, inventory, warehousing, material-handling, and packaging, and occasionally security. _____ is a channel of the supply chain which adds the value of time and place utility.

Chapter 10. Lean Production

a. 1990 Clean Air Act
b. 28-hour day
c. Third-party logistics
d. Logistics

13. A _____ is the system of organizations, people, technology, activities, information and resources involved in moving a product or service from supplier to customer. _____ activities transform natural resources, raw materials and components into a finished product that is delivered to the end customer. In sophisticated _____ systems, used products may re-enter the _____ at any point where residual value is recyclable.
   a. Drop shipping
   b. Packaging
   c. Wholesalers
   d. Supply chain

14. _____ is the management of a network of interconnected businesses involved in the ultimate provision of product and service packages required by end customers (Harland, 1996.) _____ spans all movement and storage of raw materials, work-in-process inventory, and finished goods from point of origin to point of consumption (supply chain.)

The definition an American professional association put forward is that _____ encompasses the planning and management of all activities involved in sourcing, procurement, conversion, and logistics management activities.

   a. Packaging
   b. Drop shipping
   c. Freight forwarder
   d. Supply chain management

15. _____ is a concept related to lean and just-in-time (JIT) production. The Japanese word _____ is a common term meaning 'signboard' or 'billboard'. According to Taiichi Ohno, the man credited with developing JIT, _____ is a means through which JIT is achieved.
   a. Trademark
   b. Risk management
   c. Succession planning
   d. Kanban

16. _____ is a concept in economics which refers to the extent to which an enterprise or a nation actually uses its installed productive capacity. Thus, it refers to the relationship between actual output that 'is' produced with the installed equipment and the potential output which 'could' be produced with it, if capacity was fully used.

If market demand grows, _____ will rise.

   a. Diseconomies of scale
   b. Multifactor productivity
   c. Capacity utilization
   d. Factors of production

17. _____ is the use of control systems (such as numerical control, programmable logic control, and other industrial control systems), in concert with other applications of information technology (such as computer-aided technologies [CAD, CAM, CAx]), to control industrial machinery and processes, reducing the need for human intervention. In the scope of industrialization, _____ is a step beyond mechanization. Whereas mechanization provided human operators with machinery to assist them with the physical requirements of work, _____ greatly reduces the need for human sensory and mental requirements as well.
   a. AAAI
   b. Automation
   c. A4e
   d. A Stake in the Outcome

Chapter 10. Lean Production

18. _____ is the level of inventory that minimizes the total inventory holding costs and ordering costs. The framework used to determine this order quantity is also known as Wilson _____ Model. The model was developed by F. W. Harris in 1913.

   a. Anti-leadership
   b. Effective executive
   c. Event management
   d. Economic order quantity

19. The metastability in flip-flops can be avoided by ensuring that the data and control inputs are held valid and constant for specified periods before and after the clock pulse, called the _____ and the hold time (t_h) respectively. These times are specified in the data sheet for the device, and are typically between a few nanoseconds and a few hundred picoseconds for modern devices.

Unfortunately, it is not always possible to meet the setup and hold criteria, because the flip-flop may be connected to a real-time signal that could change at any time, outside the control of the designer.

   a. 33 Strategies of War
   b. 1990 Clean Air Act
   c. 28-hour day
   d. Setup time

20. _____ has the following meanings:

The care and servicing by personnel for the purpose of maintaining equipment and facilities in satisfactory operating condition by providing for systematic inspection, detection, and correction of incipient failures either before they occur or before they develop into major defects.

   1. Maintenance, including tests, measurements, adjustments, and parts replacement, performed specifically to prevent faults from occurring.

While _____ is generally considered to be worthwhile, there are risks such as equipment failure or human error involved when performing _____, just as in any maintenance operation. _____ as scheduled overhaul or scheduled replacement provides two of the three proactive failure management policies available to the maintenance engineer. Common methods of determining what _____ failure management policies should be applied are; OEM recommendations, requirements of codes and legislation within a jurisdiction, what an 'expert' thinks ought to be done, or the maintenance that's already done to similar equipment.

   a. 28-hour day
   b. 33 Strategies of War
   c. 1990 Clean Air Act
   d. Preventive maintenance

21. In organizational development (OD), _____ is the application of Socio-Technical Systems principles and techniques to the humanization of work.

The aims of _____ to improved job satisfaction, to improved through-put, to improved quality and to reduced employee problems, e.g., grievances, absenteeism.

Under scientific management people would be directed by reason and the problems of industrial unrest would be appropriately (i.e., scientifically) addressed.

Chapter 10. Lean Production

a. Management process
c. Graduate recruitment
b. Path-goal theory
d. Work design

22. _____ is an advertisement in which a particular product specifically mentions a competitor by name for the express purpose of showing why the competitor is inferior to the product naming it.

This should not be confused with parody advertisements, where a fictional product is being advertised for the purpose of poking fun at the particular advertisement, nor should it be confused with the use of a coined brand name for the purpose of comparing the product without actually naming an actual competitor. ('Wikipedia tastes better and is less filling than the Encyclopedia Galactica.')

In the 1980s, during what has been referred to as the cola wars, soft-drink manufacturer Pepsi ran a series of advertisements where people, caught on hidden camera, in a blind taste test, chose Pepsi over rival Coca-Cola.

a. 1990 Clean Air Act
c. 28-hour day
b. 33 Strategies of War
d. Comparative advertising

23. _____ refers to training in different ways to improve overall performance. It takes advantage of the particular effectiveness of each training method, while at the same time attempting to neglect the shortcomings of that method by combining it with other methods that address its weaknesses.

Cross training is employee-employer field means, training employees to do one another's work.

a. 1990 Clean Air Act
c. 33 Strategies of War
b. Cross-training
d. 28-hour day

24. In business and engineering, _____ is the term used to describe the complete process of bringing a new product or service to market. There are two parallel paths involved in the _____ process: one involves the idea generation, product design, and detail engineering; the other involves market research and marketing analysis. Companies typically see _____ as the first stage in generating and commercializing new products within the overall strategic process of product life cycle management used to maintain or grow their market share.

a. 33 Strategies of War
c. New product development
b. 1990 Clean Air Act
d. 28-hour day

25. _____ refers to the structured transmission of data between organizations by electronic means. It is used to transfer electronic documents from one computer system to another (ie) from one trading partner to another trading partner. It is more than mere E-mail; for instance, organizations might replace bills of lading and even checks with appropriate _____ messages.

a. A4e
c. A Stake in the Outcome
b. AAAI
d. Electronic data interchange

26. _____ is used for the design, development, analysis, and optimization of technical processes and is mainly applied to chemical plants and chemical processes, but also to power stations, and similar technical facilities. Process flow diagram of a typical amine treating process used in industrial plants

Chapter 10. Lean Production

_____ is a model-based representation of chemical, physical, biological, and other technical processes and unit operations in software. Basic prerequisites are a thorough knowledge of chemical and physical properties of pure components and mixtures, of reactions, and of mathematical models which, in combination, allow the calculation of a process in computers.

a. 28-hour day
b. 33 Strategies of War
c. Process simulation
d. 1990 Clean Air Act

27. In business and engineering, new _____ is the term used to describe the complete process of bringing a new product or service to market. There are two parallel paths involved in the NProduct development process: one involves the idea generation, product design, and detail engineering; the other involves market research and marketing analysis. Companies typically see new _____ as the first stage in generating and commercializing new products within the overall strategic process of product life cycle management used to maintain or grow their market share.

a. Product development
b. 33 Strategies of War
c. 1990 Clean Air Act
d. 28-hour day

28. _____ can be considered to have three main components: quality control, quality assurance and quality improvement. _____ is focused not only on product quality, but also the means to achieve it. _____ therefore uses quality assurance and control of processes as well as products to achieve more consistent quality.

a. 1990 Clean Air Act
b. 28-hour day
c. Total quality management
d. Quality management

29. _____, in microeconomics, are the cost advantages that a business obtains due to expansion. They are factors that cause a producer's average cost per unit to fall as scale is increased. _____ is a long run concept and refers to reductions in unit cost as the size of a facility, or scale, increases.

a. A Stake in the Outcome
b. Economies of scope
c. A4e
d. Economies of scale

30. The _____ captures an expanded spectrum of values and criteria for measuring organizational success: economic, ecological and social. With the ratification of the United Nations and ICLEI _____ standard for urban and community accounting in early 2007, this became the dominant approach to public sector full cost accounting. Similar UN standards apply to natural capital and human capital measurement to assist in measurements required by _____, e.g. the ecoBudget standard for reporting ecological footprint.

a. 33 Strategies of War
b. 1990 Clean Air Act
c. 28-hour day
d. Triple bottom line

Chapter 11. Facility Location and Capacity

1. _____ is a branch of operations research concerning itself with mathematical modeling and solution of problems concerning the placement of facilities in order to minimize transportation costs, avoid placing hazardous materials near housing, outperform competitors' facilities, etc.

A simple _____ problem is the Fermat-Weber problem, in which a single facility is to be placed, with the only optimization criterion being the minimization of the sum of distances from a given set of point sites. More complex problems considered in this discipline include the placement of multiple facilities, constraints on the locations of facilities, and more complex optimization criteria.

    a. Multiscale decision making   b. 1990 Clean Air Act
    c. Facility location   d. 28-hour day

2. A _____ is a common type of chart, that represents an algorithm or process, showing the steps as boxes of various kinds, and their order by connecting these with arrows. _____s are used in analyzing, designing, documenting or managing a process or program in various fields.

The first structured method for documenting process flow, the 'flow process chart', was introduced by Frank Gilbreth to members of ASME in 1921 as the presentation 'Process Charts--First Steps in Finding the One Best Way'.

    a. 1990 Clean Air Act   b. Flowchart
    c. 33 Strategies of War   d. 28-hour day

3. _____ is, in very basic words, a position a firm occupies against its competitors.

According to Michael Porter, the three methods for creating a sustainable _____ are through:

1. Cost leadership

2. Differentiation

3. Focus (economics)

    a. Competitive advantage   b. 28-hour day
    c. 1990 Clean Air Act   d. Theory Z

4. An _____ is a manufacturing process in which parts (usually interchangeable parts) are added to a product in a sequential manner using optimally planned logistics to create a finished product much faster than with handcrafting-type methods. The _____ developed by Ford Motor Company between 1908 and 1915 made _____s famous in the following decade through the social ramifications of mass production, such as the affordability of the Ford Model T and the introduction of high wages for Ford workers. However, the various preconditions for the development at Ford stretched far back into the 19th century, from the gradual realization of the dream of interchangeability, to the concept of reinventing workflow and job descriptions using analytical methods.

    a. Assembly line   b. AAAI
    c. A Stake in the Outcome   d. A4e

Chapter 11. Facility Location and Capacity

5. In economics, business, retail, and accounting, a _____ is the value of money that has been used up to produce something, and hence is not available for use anymore. In economics, a _____ is an alternative that is given up as a result of a decision. In business, the _____ may be one of acquisition, in which case the amount of money expended to acquire it is counted as _____.

   a. Cost overrun
   b. Fixed costs
   c. Cost allocation
   d. Cost

6. In organizational development (OD), _____ is the application of Socio-Technical Systems principles and techniques to the humanization of work.

The aims of _____ to improved job satisfaction, to improved through-put, to improved quality and to reduced employee problems, e.g., grievances, absenteeism.

Under scientific management people would be directed by reason and the problems of industrial unrest would be appropriately (i.e., scientifically) addressed.

   a. Work design
   b. Management process
   c. Path-goal theory
   d. Graduate recruitment

7. _____ or lean production, which is often known simply as 'Lean', is a production practice that considers the expenditure of resources for any goal other than the creation of value for the end customer to be wasteful, and thus a target for elimination. Working from the perspective of the customer who consumes a product or service, 'value' is defined as any action or process that a customer would be willing to pay for. Basically, lean is centered around creating more value with less work.

   a. Six Sigma
   b. Production line
   c. Theory of constraints
   d. Lean manufacturing

8. The _____ is a trilateral trade bloc in North America created by the governments of the United States, Canada, and Mexico. The agreement creating the trade bloc came into force on January 1, 1994. It superseded the Canada-United States Free Trade Agreement between the U.S. and Canada.

   a. Trade union
   b. Career portfolios
   c. Business war game
   d. North American Free Trade Agreement

9. _____ is an advertisement in which a particular product specifically mentions a competitor by name for the express purpose of showing why the competitor is inferior to the product naming it.

This should not be confused with parody advertisements, where a fictional product is being advertised for the purpose of poking fun at the particular advertisement, nor should it be confused with the use of a coined brand name for the purpose of comparing the product without actually naming an actual competitor. ('Wikipedia tastes better and is less filling than the Encyclopedia Galactica.')

In the 1980s, during what has been referred to as the cola wars, soft-drink manufacturer Pepsi ran a series of advertisements where people, caught on hidden camera, in a blind taste test, chose Pepsi over rival Coca-Cola.

Chapter 11. Facility Location and Capacity

a. 28-hour day
b. 1990 Clean Air Act
c. 33 Strategies of War
d. Comparative advertising

10. _____ is a costing model that identifies activities in an organization and assigns the cost of each activity resource to all products and services according to the actual consumption by each: it assigns more indirect costs (overhead) into direct costs.

In this way an organization can establish the true cost of its individual products and services for the purposes of identifying and eliminating those which are unprofitable and lowering the prices of those which are overpriced.

In a business organization, the ABC methodology assigns an organization's resource costs through activities to the products and services provided to its customers.

a. Indirect costs
b. A4e
c. A Stake in the Outcome
d. Activity-based costing

11. A _____ or business method is a collection of related, structured activities or tasks that produce a specific service or product (serve a particular goal) for a particular customer or customers. It often can be visualized with a flowchart as a sequence of activities.

There are three types of _____es:

1. Management processes, the processes that govern the operation of a system. Typical management processes include 'Corporate Governance' and 'Strategic Management'.
2. Operational processes, processes that constitute the core business and create the primary value stream. Typical operational processes are Purchasing, Manufacturing, Marketing, and Sales.
3. Supporting processes, which support the core processes. Examples include Accounting, Recruitment, Technical support.

A _____ begins with a customer's need and ends with a customer's need fulfillment. Process oriented organizations break down the barriers of structural departments and try to avoid functional silos.

a. 1990 Clean Air Act
b. Business process
c. 33 Strategies of War
d. 28-hour day

12. _____ refers to training in different ways to improve overall performance. It takes advantage of the particular effectiveness of each training method, while at the same time attempting to neglect the shortcomings of that method by combining it with other methods that address its weaknesses.

Cross training is employee-employer field means, training employees to do one another's work.

a. 28-hour day
b. 1990 Clean Air Act
c. 33 Strategies of War
d. Cross-training

Chapter 11. Facility Location and Capacity

13. _____ is one of the four elements of marketing mix. An organization or set of organizations (go-betweens) involved in the process of making a product or service available for use or consumption by a consumer or business user.

The other three parts of the marketing mix are product, pricing, and promotion.

a. Distribution
c. Job creation programs
b. Missing completely at random
d. Matching theory

14. A _____ is a document that captures and agrees the work activities, deliverables and timeline that a vendor will execute against in performance of work for a customer. Detailed requirements and pricing are usually specified in a _____, along with many other terms and conditions.

There are many formats and styles of _____ document templates that have been specialized for the Hardware or Software solutions being described in the Request for Proposal.

a. 1990 Clean Air Act
c. Modular design
b. 28-hour day
d. Statement of work

15. In finance, the _____s between two currencies specifies how much one currency is worth in terms of the other. It is the value of a foreign nation's currency in terms of the home nation's currency. For example an _____ of 102 Japanese yen to the United States dollar means that JPY 102 is worth the same as USD 1.

a. AAAI
c. A Stake in the Outcome
b. A4e
d. Exchange rate

16. In quality assessment, _____ is an inspection standard describing the maximum number of defects that could be considered acceptable during the random sampling of an inspection. The defects found during inspection are classified into three levels: critical, major and minor. Broadly, these levels are defined as follows:

- Critical defects are those that render the product unsafe or hazardous for the end user, or that contravene mandatory regulations.

- Major defects can result in the product's failure, reducing its marketability, usability, or saleability.

- Minor defects do not affect the product's marketability or usability, but represent workmanship defects that make the product fall short of defined quality standards.

Different companies maintain different interpretations of each defect type.

a. Acceptable quality level
c. AAAI
b. A Stake in the Outcome
d. A4e

17. _____ is subcontracting a process, such as product design or manufacturing, to a third-party company. The decision to outsource is often made in the interest of lowering cost or making better use of time and energy costs, redirecting or conserving energy directed at the competencies of a particular business, or to make more efficient use of land, labor, capital, (information) technology and resources. _____ became part of the business lexicon during the 1980s.

a. Opinion leadership
b. Unemployment insurance
c. Operant conditioning
d. Outsourcing

18. Manufacturing Resource Planning (_____) is defined by APICS as a method for the effective planning of all resources of a manufacturing company. Ideally, it addresses operational planning in units, financial planning in dollars, and has a simulation capability to answer 'what-if' questions and extension of closed-loop MRP. Manufacturing Resource Planning (or MRP2) - Around 1980, over-frequent changes in sales forecasts, entailing continual readjustments in production, as well as the unsuitability of the parameters fixed by the system, led MRP (Material Requirement Planning) to evolve into a new concept : Manufacturing Resource Planning (e.g. MRP 2)

This is not exclusively a software function, but a marriage of people skills, dedication to data base accuracy, and computer resources.

a. Jidoka
b. MRP II
c. Homeworkers
d. Manufacturing resource planning

19. A _____ for a set of products is a warehouse or other specialized building, often with refrigeration or air conditioning, which is stocked with products (goods) to be re-distributed to retailers, wholesalers or directly to consumers. A _____ is a principle part, the 'order processing' element, of the entire 'order fulfillment' process. _____s are usually thought of as being 'demand driven'.

a. Third-party logistics
b. Distribution center
c. 28-hour day
d. 1990 Clean Air Act

20. _____, in microeconomics, are the cost advantages that a business obtains due to expansion. They are factors that cause a producer's average cost per unit to fall as scale is increased. _____ is a long run concept and refers to reductions in unit cost as the size of a facility, or scale, increases.

a. Economies of scope
b. A Stake in the Outcome
c. Economies of scale
d. A4e

21. _____ consists of the sale of goods or merchandise from a fixed location, such as a department store, boutique or kiosk in small or individual lots for direct consumption by the purchaser. _____ may include subordinated services, such as delivery. Purchasers may be individuals or businesses.

a. 1990 Clean Air Act
b. 28-hour day
c. Planogram
d. Retailing

22. _____ is a concept in economics which refers to the extent to which an enterprise or a nation actually uses its installed productive capacity. Thus, it refers to the relationship between actual output that 'is' produced with the installed equipment and the potential output which 'could' be produced with it, if capacity was fully used.

If market demand grows, _____ will rise.

a. Diseconomies of scale
b. Factors of production
c. Multifactor productivity
d. Capacity utilization

23. _____ measures the performance of a system. Certain goals are defined and the _____ gives the percentage to which they should be achieved.

Chapter 11. Facility Location and Capacity

Examples

- Percentage of calls answered in a call center.
- Percentage of customers waiting less than a given fixed time.
- Percentage of customers that do not experience a stock out.

_____ is used in supply chain management and in inventory management to measure the performance of inventory systems.

Under stochastic conditions it is unavoidable that in some periods the inventory on hand is not sufficient to deliver the complete demand and, as a consequence, that part of the demand is filled only after an inventory-related waiting time.

a. 1990 Clean Air Act
b. 33 Strategies of War
c. 28-hour day
d. Service level

24. In queueing theory, _____ is the proportion of the system's resources which is used by the traffic which arrives at it. It should be strictly less than one for the system to function well. It is usually represented by the symbol ρ.
a. A4e
b. Utilization
c. A Stake in the Outcome
d. AAAI

25. _____ are the forces that cause larger firms to produce goods and services at increased per-unit costs. They are less well known than what economists have long understood as 'economies of scale', the forces which enable larger firms to produce goods and services at reduced per-unit costs.

Some of the forces which cause a diseconomy of scale are listed below:

Ideally, all employees of a firm would have one-on-one communication with each other so they know exactly what the other workers are doing.

a. Multifactor productivity
b. Production function
c. Factors of production
d. Diseconomies of scale

26. _____ is a term applied to an organization that has created the processes, tools, and training to enable it to respond quickly to customer needs and market changes while still controlling costs and quality.

An enabling factor in becoming an agile manufacturer has been the development of manufacturing support technology that allows the marketers, the designers and the production personnel to share a common database of parts and products, to share data on production capacities and problems -- particularly where small initial problems may have larger downstream effects. It is a general proposition of manufacturing that the cost of correcting quality issues increases as the problem moves downstream, so that it is cheaper to correct quality problems at the earliest possible point in the process.

a. A Stake in the Outcome
c. AAAI
b. Agile manufacturing
d. A4e

27. _____ is the process of estimation in unknown situations. Prediction is a similar, but more general term. Both can refer to estimation of time series, cross-sectional or longitudinal data.
   a. 33 Strategies of War
   b. 28-hour day
   c. 1990 Clean Air Act
   d. Forecasting

28. _____ is a diversified financial services company with operations around the world. Wells Fargo is the fourth largest bank in the US by assets and the second largest bank by market cap.
   a. Holding company
   b. Process-based management
   c. Committee for Economic Development
   d. Wells Fargo ' Co.

Chapter 12. Facility Layouts

1. An _____ is a manufacturing process in which parts (usually interchangeable parts) are added to a product in a sequential manner using optimally planned logistics to create a finished product much faster than with handcrafting-type methods. The _____ developed by Ford Motor Company between 1908 and 1915 made _____s famous in the following decade through the social ramifications of mass production, such as the affordability of the Ford Model T and the introduction of high wages for Ford workers. However, the various preconditions for the development at Ford stretched far back into the 19th century, from the gradual realization of the dream of interchangeability, to the concept of reinventing workflow and job descriptions using analytical methods.
    a. A Stake in the Outcome
    b. A4e
    c. AAAI
    d. Assembly line

2. _____ are typically small manufacturing operations that handle specialized manufacturing processes such as small customer orders or small batch jobs. _____ typically move on to different jobs (possibly with different customers) when each job is completed. By nature of this type of manufacturing operation, _____ are usually specialized in skill and processes.
    a. 33 Strategies of War
    b. 1990 Clean Air Act
    c. 28-hour day
    d. Job shops

3. _____ is one of the managerial functions like planning, organizing, staffing and directing. It is an important function because it helps to check the errors and to take the corrective action so that deviation from standards are minimized and stated goals of the organization are achieved in desired manner. According to modern concepts, _____ is a foreseeing action whereas earlier concept of _____ was used only when errors were detected. _____ in management means setting standards, measuring actual performance and taking corrective action.
    a. Decision tree pruning
    b. Control
    c. Schedule of reinforcement
    d. Turnover

4. _____ is an advertisement in which a particular product specifically mentions a competitor by name for the express purpose of showing why the competitor is inferior to the product naming it.

This should not be confused with parody advertisements, where a fictional product is being advertised for the purpose of poking fun at the particular advertisement, nor should it be confused with the use of a coined brand name for the purpose of comparing the product without actually naming an actual competitor. ('Wikipedia tastes better and is less filling than the Encyclopedia Galactica.')

In the 1980s, during what has been referred to as the cola wars, soft-drink manufacturer Pepsi ran a series of advertisements where people, caught on hidden camera, in a blind taste test, chose Pepsi over rival Coca-Cola.

    a. 33 Strategies of War
    b. 28-hour day
    c. 1990 Clean Air Act
    d. Comparative advertising

5. _____ can be defined as the maximum time per unit allowed to produce a product in order to meet demand. It is derived from the German word Taktzeit which translates to cycle time. _____ sets the pace for industrial manufacturing lines. In automobile manufacturing, for example, cars are assembled on a line, and are moved on to the next station after a certain time - the _____. Therefore, the time needed to complete work on each station has to be less than the _____ in order for the product to be completed within the alloted time.
    a. Six Sigma
    b. Production line
    c. Theory of constraints
    d. Takt time

6. _____ is the process of estimation in unknown situations. Prediction is a similar, but more general term. Both can refer to estimation of time series, cross-sectional or longitudinal data.
   a. 1990 Clean Air Act
   b. 33 Strategies of War
   c. 28-hour day
   d. Forecasting

7. In statistics, signal processing, and many other fields, a _____ is a sequence of data points, measured typically at successive times, spaced at (often uniform) time intervals. _____ analysis comprises methods that attempt to understand such _____, often either to understand the underlying context of the data points (Where did they come from? What generated them?), or to make forecasts (predictions.) _____ forecasting is the use of a model to forecast future events based on known past events: to forecast future data points before they are measured.
   a. Standard deviation
   b. Histogram
   c. Moving average
   d. Time series

8. In statistics, signal processing, and many other fields, a time series is a sequence of data points, measured typically at successive times, spaced at (often uniform) time intervals. _____ comprises methods that attempt to understand such time series, often either to understand the underlying context of the data points (Where did they come from? What generated them?), or to make forecasts (predictions.) Time series forecasting is the use of a model to forecast future events based on known past events: to forecast future data points before they are measured.
   a. Time series analysis
   b. Moving average
   c. Failure rate
   d. Correlation

9. In economics, business, retail, and accounting, a _____ is the value of money that has been used up to produce something, and hence is not available for use anymore. In economics, a _____ is an alternative that is given up as a result of a decision. In business, the _____ may be one of acquisition, in which case the amount of money expended to acquire it is counted as _____.
   a. Fixed costs
   b. Cost overrun
   c. Cost
   d. Cost allocation

10. _____, a business term, is a measure of how products and services supplied by a company meet or surpass customer expectation. It is seen as a key performance indicator within business and is part of the four perspectives of a Balanced Scorecard.

In a competitive marketplace where businesses compete for customers, _____ is seen as a key differentiator and increasingly has become a key element of business strategy.

   a. Customer satisfaction
   b. Foreign ownership
   c. Critical Success Factor
   d. Horizontal integration

11. The _____ is a systematic, interactive forecasting method which relies on a panel of independent experts. The carefully selected experts answer questionnaires in two or more rounds. After each round, a facilitator provides an anonymous summary of the experts' forecasts from the previous round as well as the reasons they provided for their judgments.
    a. Hoshin Kanri
    b. Delphi method
    c. Quality function deployment
    d. Learning organization

12. In statistics, _____ is a technique that can be applied to time series data, either to produce smoothed data for presentation, or to make forecasts. The time series data themselves are a sequence of observations. The observed phenomenon may be an essentially random process, or it may be an orderly, but noisy, process.
   a. Exponential smoothing
   b. A Stake in the Outcome
   c. AAAI
   d. A4e

13. In economics, _____s are key economic variables that economists used to predict a new phase of the business cycle. A _____ is one that changes before the economy does; a lagging indicator is one that changes after the economy has changed. Examples of _____s include stock prices, which often improve or worsen before a similar change in the economy.
   a. Perfect competition
   b. Leading indicator
   c. Human capital
   d. Deflation

14. In statistics, _____ is used for two things:

   - to construct a simple formula that will predict a value or values for a variable given the value of another variable.
   - to test whether and how a given variable is related to another variable or variables.

   _____ is a form of regression analysis in which the relationship between one or more independent variables and another variable, called the dependent variable, is modelled by a least squares function, called a _____ equation. This function is a linear combination of one or more model parameters, called regression coefficients. A _____ equation with one independent variable represents a straight line when the predicted value (i.e. the dependent variable from the regression equation) is plotted against the independent variable: this is called a simple _____. However, note that 'linear' does not refer to this straight line, but rather to the way in which the regression coefficients occur in the regression equation.

   a. Linear regression
   b. Clinical decision support systems
   c. Strict liability
   d. Continuous

15. Marketing research is a form of business research and is generally divided into two categories: consumer _____ and business-to-business (B2B) _____, which was previously known as industrial marketing research. Consumer marketing research studies the buying habits of individual people while business-to-business marketing research investigates the markets for products sold by one business to another.

   Consumer _____ is a form of applied sociology that concentrates on understanding the behaviours, whims and preferences, of consumers in a market-based economy, and aims to understand the effects and comparative success of marketing campaigns.

   a. Mystery shoppers
   b. Questionnaire
   c. Market research
   d. Questionnaire construction

16. In statistics, a _____ rolling mean or running average, is a type of finite impulse response filter used to analyze a set of data points by creating a series of averages of different subsets of the full data set. A _____ is not a single number, but it is a set of numbers, each of which is the average of the corresponding subset of a larger set of data points. A _____ may also use unequal weights for each data value in the subset to emphasize particular values in the subset.

Chapter 12. Facility Layouts

a. Standard deviation
c. Homoscedastic
b. Time series analysis
d. Moving average

17. In statistics, _____ refers to techniques for the modeling and analysis of numerical data consisting of values of a dependent variable and of one or more independent variables The dependent variable in the regression equation is modeled as a function of the independent variables, corresponding parameters, and an error term. The error term is treated as a random variable and represents unexplained variation in the dependent variable.

a. Stepwise regression
c. Least squares
b. Trend analysis
d. Regression analysis

18. A _____ is the unweighted mean of the previous n data points. For example, a 10-day _____ of closing price is the mean of the previous 10 days' closing prices. If those prices are $p_M, p_{M-1}, \ldots, p_{M-9}$ then the formula is

$$SMA = \frac{p_M + p_{M-1} + \cdots + p_{M-9}}{10}$$

When calculating successive values, a new value comes into the sum and an old value drops out, meaning a full summation each time is unnecessary,

$$SMA_{\text{today}} = SMA_{\text{yesterday}} - \frac{p_{M-n}}{n} + \frac{p_M}{n}$$

In technical analysis there are various popular values for n, like 10 days, 40 days, or 200 days.

a. Simple moving average
c. Statistically significant
b. Descriptive statistics
d. Confidence interval

19. The term '_____' refers to the concept of collecting information and attempting to spot a pattern in the information. In some fields of study, the term '_____' has more formally-defined meanings.

In project management _____ is a mathematical technique that uses historical results to predict future outcome.

a. Least squares
c. Trend analysis
b. Stepwise regression
d. Regression analysis

20. _____ of the learning curve effect and the closely related experience curve effect express the relationship between equations for experience and efficiency or between efficiency gains and investment in the effort. The experience of 'learning curves' was first observed by the 19th Century German psychologist Hermann Ebbinghaus according to the difficulty of memorizing varying numbers of verbal stimuli, and subsequent learning about the complex processes of learning are discussed in the

Chapter 12. Facility Layouts

The rule used for representing the learning curve effect states that the more times a task has been performed, the less time will be required on each subsequent iteration.

- a. Distribution
- b. Models
- c. Point biserial correlation coefficient
- d. Spatial Decision Support Systems

21. In statistics and image processing, to smooth a data set is to create an approximating function that attempts to capture important patterns in the data, while leaving out noise or other fine-scale structures/rapid phenomena. Many different algorithms are used in _____. One of the most common algorithms is the 'moving average', often used to try to capture important trends in repeated statistical surveys.
    - a. 33 Strategies of War
    - b. 1990 Clean Air Act
    - c. 28-hour day
    - d. Smoothing

22. In economics, _____ is the desire to own something and the ability to pay for it. The term _____ signifies the ability or the willingness to buy a particular commodity at a given point of time.
    - a. 28-hour day
    - b. 33 Strategies of War
    - c. 1990 Clean Air Act
    - d. Demand

23. A _____ or business method is a collection of related, structured activities or tasks that produce a specific service or product (serve a particular goal) for a particular customer or customers. It often can be visualized with a flowchart as a sequence of activities.

There are three types of _____ es:

1. Management processes, the processes that govern the operation of a system. Typical management processes include 'Corporate Governance' and 'Strategic Management'.
2. Operational processes, processes that constitute the core business and create the primary value stream. Typical operational processes are Purchasing, Manufacturing, Marketing, and Sales.
3. Supporting processes, which support the core processes. Examples include Accounting, Recruitment, Technical support.

A _____ begins with a customer's need and ends with a customer's need fulfillment. Process oriented organizations break down the barriers of structural departments and try to avoid functional silos.

- a. 1990 Clean Air Act
- b. 28-hour day
- c. Business process
- d. 33 Strategies of War

24. The _____ is given by the United States National Institute of Standards and Technology. Through the actions of the National Productivity Advisory Committee chaired by Jack Grayson, it was established by the Malcolm Baldrige National Quality Improvement Act of 1987 - Public Law 100-107 and named for Malcolm Baldrige, who served as United States Secretary of Commerce during the Reagan administration from 1981 until his 1987 death in a rodeo accident. APQC, , organized the first White House Conference on Productivity, spearheading the creation and design of the _____ in 1987, and jointly administering the award for its first three years.

98   Chapter 12. Facility Layouts

a. Scenario planning
c. Business Network Transformation
b. Time and attendance
d. Malcolm Baldrige National Quality Award

25. _____ is a business management strategy aimed at embedding awareness of quality in all organizational processes. _____ has been widely used in manufacturing, education, hospitals, call centers, government, and service industries, as well as NASA space and science programs.

As defined by the International Organization for Standardization (ISO):

'_____ is a management approach for an organization, centered on quality, based on the participation of all its members and aiming at long-term success through customer satisfaction, and benefits to all members of the organization and to society.' ISO 8402:1994

One major aim is to reduce variation from every process so that greater consistency of effort is obtained. (Royse, D., Thyer, B., Padgett D., ' Logan T., 2006)

a. 1990 Clean Air Act
c. 28-hour day
b. Quality management
d. Total quality management

26. In statistics, _____ is:

- the arithmetic _____
- the expected value of a random variable, which is also called the population _____.

It is sometimes stated that the '_____' _____s average. This is incorrect if '_____' is taken in the specific sense of 'arithmetic _____' as there are different types of averages: the _____, median, and mode. Other simple statistical analyses use measures of spread, such as range, interquartile range, or standard deviation. For a real-valued random variable X, the _____ is the expectation of X. Note that not every probability distribution has a defined _____; see the Cauchy distribution for an example.

a. Control chart
c. Correlation
b. Statistical inference
d. Mean

27. _____ is measure of accuracy in a fitted time series value in statistics, specifically trending. It usually expresses accuracy as a percentage.

$$\text{MAPE} = \frac{1}{n}\sum_{t=1}^{n}\left|\frac{A_t - F_t}{A_t}\right|$$

The difference between actual value A_t and the forecast value F_t, is divided by the actual value A_t again.

a. 33 Strategies of War
c. 1990 Clean Air Act
b. 28-hour day
d. Mean absolute percentage error

Chapter 12. Facility Layouts

28. The method of _____ is used to approximately solve overdetermined systems, i.e. systems of equations in which there are more equations than unknowns. _____ is often applied in statistical contexts, particularly regression analysis.

_____ can be interpreted as a method of fitting data.

a. Stepwise regression
b. Regression analysis
c. Trend analysis
d. Least squares

29. In statistics, the _____, R^2 is used in the context of statistical models whose main purpose is the prediction of future outcomes on the basis of other related information. It is the proportion of variability in a data set that is accounted for by the statistical model. It provides a measure of how well future outcomes are likely to be predicted by the model.
a. Stepwise regression
b. Trend analysis
c. Regression analysis
d. Coefficient of determination

30. In statistics, the _____ of an estimator is one of many ways to quantify the amount by which an estimator differs from the true value of the quantity being estimated. As a loss function, _____ is called squared error loss. _____ measures the average of the square of the 'error.' The error is the amount by which the estimator differs from the quantity to be estimated.
a. 1990 Clean Air Act
b. 28-hour day
c. Mean squared error
d. 33 Strategies of War

31. _____ is the process of understanding, anticipating and influencing consumer behavior in order to maximize revenue or profits from a fixed, perishable resource This process was first discovered by Dr. Matt H. Keller. The challenge is to sell the right resources to the right customer at the right time for the right price.
a. Yield management
b. Business model design
c. Gap analysis
d. Business networking

32. _____ is, in very basic words, a position a firm occupies against its competitors.

According to Michael Porter, the three methods for creating a sustainable _____ are through:

1. Cost leadership

2. Differentiation

3. Focus (economics)

a. 1990 Clean Air Act
b. 28-hour day
c. Theory Z
d. Competitive advantage

33. In queueing theory, _____ is the proportion of the system's resources which is used by the traffic which arrives at it. It should be strictly less than one for the system to function well. It is usually represented by the symbol ρ.
a. A Stake in the Outcome
b. Utilization
c. AAAI
d. A4e

Chapter 13. Aggregate Planning

1. _____ is the process of estimation in unknown situations. Prediction is a similar, but more general term. Both can refer to estimation of time series, cross-sectional or longitudinal data.
   a. 33 Strategies of War
   b. 28-hour day
   c. 1990 Clean Air Act
   d. Forecasting

2. _____ is an organization's process of defining its strategy and making decisions on allocating its resources to pursue this strategy, including its capital and people. Various business analysis techniques can be used in _____, including SWOT analysis (Strengths, Weaknesses, Opportunities, and Threats) and PEST analysis (Political, Economic, Social, and Technological analysis) or STEER analysis involving Socio-cultural, Technological, Economic, Ecological, and Regulatory factors and EPISTEL (Environment, Political, Informatic, Social, Technological, Economic and Legal)

   _____ is the formal consideration of an organization's future course. All _____ deals with at least one of three key questions:

   1. 'What do we do?'
   2. 'For whom do we do it?'
   3. 'How do we excel?'

   In business _____, the third question is better phrased 'How can we beat or avoid competition?'. (Bradford and Duncan, page 1.)

   a. 33 Strategies of War
   b. 1990 Clean Air Act
   c. Strategic planning
   d. 28-hour day

3. _____ generally refers to a list of all planned expenses and revenues. It is a plan for saving and spending. A _____ is an important concept in microeconomics, which uses a _____ line to illustrate the trade-offs between two or more goods.
   a. 33 Strategies of War
   b. Budget
   c. 1990 Clean Air Act
   d. 28-hour day

4. A _____ is a plan for production, staffing, inventory, etc. It is usually linked to manufacturing where the plan indicates when and how much of each product will be demanded. This plan quantifies significant processes, parts, and other resources in order to optimize production, to identify bottlenecks, and to anticipate needs and completed goods.
   a. Value engineering
   b. Remanufacturing
   c. Master production schedule
   d. Piecework

5. In statistics, signal processing, and many other fields, a _____ is a sequence of data points, measured typically at successive times, spaced at (often uniform) time intervals. _____ analysis comprises methods that attempt to understand such _____, often either to understand the underlying context of the data points (Where did they come from? What generated them?), or to make forecasts (predictions.) _____ forecasting is the use of a model to forecast future events based on known past events: to forecast future data points before they are measured.
   a. Moving average
   b. Histogram
   c. Standard deviation
   d. Time series

6. In statistics, signal processing, and many other fields, a time series is a sequence of data points, measured typically at successive times, spaced at (often uniform) time intervals. _____ comprises methods that attempt to understand such time series, often either to understand the underlying context of the data points (Where did they come from? What generated them?), or to make forecasts (predictions.) Time series forecasting is the use of a model to forecast future events based on known past events: to forecast future data points before they are measured.

    a. Correlation   b. Moving average

    c. Time series analysis   d. Failure rate

7. _____ is the process of determining the production capacity needed by an organization to meet changing demands for its products. In the context of _____, 'capacity' is the maximum amount of work that an organization is capable of completing in a given period of time.

A discrepancy between the capacity of an organization and the demands of its customers results in inefficiency, either in under-utilized resources or unfulfilled customers.

    a. Scientific management   b. Remanufacturing

    c. Productivity   d. Capacity planning

8. In microeconomics, industrial organization is the field which describes the behavior of firms in the marketplace with regard to production, pricing, employment and other decisions. _____ in this field range from classical issues such as opportunity cost to neoclassical concepts such as factors of production.

- Production theory basics
    - production efficiency
    - factors of production
    - total, average, and marginal product curves
    - marginal productivity
    - isoquants ' isocosts
    - the marginal rate of technical substitution
- Economic rent
    - classical factor rents
    - Paretian factor rents
- Production possibility frontier
    - what products are possible given a set of resources
    - the trade-off between producing one product rather than another
    - the marginal rate of transformation
- Production function
    - inputs
    - diminishing returns to inputs
    - the stages of production
    - shifts in a production function
- Cost theory
    - the different types of costs
        - opportunity cost
        - accounting cost or historical costs
        - transaction cost
        - sunk cost
        - marginal cost
    - the isocost line
- Cost-of-production theory of value
- Long-run cost and production functions
    - long-run average cost
    - long-run production function and efficiency
    - returns to scale and isoclines
    - minimum efficient scale
    - plant capacity
- Economies of density
- Economies of scale
    - the efficiency consequences of increasing or decreasing the level of production
- Economies of scope
    - the efficiency consequences of increasing or decreasing the number of different types of products produced, promoted, and distributed
- Optimum factor allocation
    - output elasticity of factor costs
    - marginal revenue product
    - marginal resource cost
- Pricing
    - various aspects of the pricing decision
- Transfer pricing
    - selling within a multi-divisional company
- Joint product pricing
    - price setting when two products are linked
- Price discrimination

- different prices to different buyers
- types of price discrimination
- yield management
- Price skimming
  - price discrimination over time
- Two part tariffs
  - charging a price composed of two parts, usually an initial fee and an ongoing fee
- Price points
  - the effects of a non-linear demand curve on pricing
- Cost-plus pricing
  - a markup is applied to a cost term in order to calculate price
  - cost-plus pricing with elasticity considerations
  - cost plus pricing is often used along with break even analysis
- Rate of return pricing
  - calculate price based on the required rate of return on investment, or rate of return on sales
- Profit maximization
  - determining the optimum price and quantity
  - the totals approach
  - marginal approach of production

Chapter 13. Aggregate Planning

a. Pricing	b. Markup
c. Topics	d. Price floor

9. A _____ is an assignment of a probability to each pure strategy. This allows for a player to randomly select a pure strategy. Since probabilities are continuous, there are infinitely many mixed strategies available to a player, even if their strategy set is finite.

a. Complete information	b. Global games
c. Perfect information	d. Mixed strategy

10. A _____ is the system of organizations, people, technology, activities, information and resources involved in moving a product or service from supplier to customer. _____ activities transform natural resources, raw materials and components into a finished product that is delivered to the end customer. In sophisticated _____ systems, used products may re-enter the _____ at any point where residual value is recyclable.

a. Packaging	b. Supply chain
c. Wholesalers	d. Drop shipping

11. _____ is the management of a network of interconnected businesses involved in the ultimate provision of product and service packages required by end customers (Harland, 1996.) _____ spans all movement and storage of raw materials, work-in-process inventory, and finished goods from point of origin to point of consumption (supply chain.)

The definition an American professional association put forward is that _____ encompasses the planning and management of all activities involved in sourcing, procurement, conversion, and logistics management activities.

a. Supply chain management	b. Drop shipping
c. Freight forwarder	d. Packaging

12. In economics, business, retail, and accounting, a _____ is the value of money that has been used up to produce something, and hence is not available for use anymore. In economics, a _____ is an alternative that is given up as a result of a decision. In business, the _____ may be one of acquisition, in which case the amount of money expended to acquire it is counted as _____.

a. Cost allocation	b. Cost overrun
c. Cost	d. Fixed costs

13. _____ is a costing model that identifies activities in an organization and assigns the cost of each activity resource to all products and services according to the actual consumption by each: it assigns more indirect costs (overhead) into direct costs.

In this way an organization can establish the true cost of its individual products and services for the purposes of identifying and eliminating those which are unprofitable and lowering the prices of those which are overpriced.

In a business organization, the ABC methodology assigns an organization's resource costs through activities to the products and services provided to its customers.

a. Indirect costs
b. A Stake in the Outcome
c. A4e
d. Activity-based costing

14. An _____ is a manufacturing process in which parts (usually interchangeable parts) are added to a product in a sequential manner using optimally planned logistics to create a finished product much faster than with handcrafting-type methods. The _____ developed by Ford Motor Company between 1908 and 1915 made _____s famous in the following decade through the social ramifications of mass production, such as the affordability of the Ford Model T and the introduction of high wages for Ford workers. However, the various preconditions for the development at Ford stretched far back into the 19th century, from the gradual realization of the dream of interchangeability, to the concept of reinventing workflow and job descriptions using analytical methods.
   a. Assembly line
   b. A Stake in the Outcome
   c. A4e
   d. AAAI

15. _____ or lean production, which is often known simply as 'Lean', is a production practice that considers the expenditure of resources for any goal other than the creation of value for the end customer to be wasteful, and thus a target for elimination. Working from the perspective of the customer who consumes a product or service, 'value' is defined as any action or process that a customer would be willing to pay for. Basically, lean is centered around creating more value with less work.
   a. Production line
   b. Six Sigma
   c. Theory of constraints
   d. Lean manufacturing

16. _____ is measure of accuracy in a fitted time series value in statistics, specifically trending. It usually expresses accuracy as a percentage.

$$\text{MAPE} = \frac{1}{n}\sum_{t=1}^{n}\left|\frac{A_t - F_t}{A_t}\right|$$

The difference between actual value A_t and the forecast value F_t, is divided by the actual value A_t again.

   a. 33 Strategies of War
   b. 28-hour day
   c. 1990 Clean Air Act
   d. Mean absolute percentage error

17. In economics and finance, _____ is the change in total cost that arises when the quantity produced changes by one unit. It is the cost of producing one more unit of a good. Mathematically, the _____ function is expressed as the first derivative of the total cost (TC) function with respect to quantity (Q.)
   a. Transaction cost
   b. Cost overrun
   c. Variable cost
   d. Marginal Cost

18. _____ is an advertisement in which a particular product specifically mentions a competitor by name for the express purpose of showing why the competitor is inferior to the product naming it.

This should not be confused with parody advertisements, where a fictional product is being advertised for the purpose of poking fun at the particular advertisement, nor should it be confused with the use of a coined brand name for the purpose of comparing the product without actually naming an actual competitor. ('Wikipedia tastes better and is less filling than the Encyclopedia Galactica.')

Chapter 13. Aggregate Planning

In the 1980s, during what has been referred to as the cola wars, soft-drink manufacturer Pepsi ran a series of advertisements where people, caught on hidden camera, in a blind taste test, chose Pepsi over rival Coca-Cola.

- a. 33 Strategies of War
- b. Comparative advertising
- c. 1990 Clean Air Act
- d. 28-hour day

19. _____ is an operational activity which does an aggregate plan for the production process, in advance of 2 to 18 months, to give an idea to management as to what quantity of materials and other resources are to be procured and when, so that the total cost of operations of the organization is kept to the minimum over that period.

The quantity of outsourcing, subcontracting of items, overtime of labor, numbers to be hired and fired in each period and the amount of inventory to be held in stock and to be backlogged for each period are decided. All of these activities are done within the framework of the company ethics, policies, and long term commitment to the society, community and the country of operation.

- a. A Stake in the Outcome
- b. Earned Schedule
- c. Aggregate planning
- d. Earned value management

20. _____ is the process of understanding, anticipating and influencing consumer behavior in order to maximize revenue or profits from a fixed, perishable resource This process was first discovered by Dr. Matt H. Keller. The challenge is to sell the right resources to the right customer at the right time for the right price.
- a. Business model design
- b. Business networking
- c. Yield management
- d. Gap analysis

21. A _____ is a group of people or organizations sharing one or more characteristics that cause them to have similar product and/or service needs. A true _____ meets all of the following criteria: it is distinct from other segments (different segments have different needs), it is homogeneous within the segment (exhibits common needs); it responds similarly to a market stimulus, and it can be reached by a market intervention. The term is also used when consumers with identical product and/or service needs are divided up into groups so they can be charged different amounts.
- a. Context analysis
- b. Customer relationship management
- c. Market segment
- d. SWOT analysis

22. In economics, _____ are business expenses that are not dependent on the activities of the business They tend to be time-related, such as salaries or rents being paid per month. This is in contrast to variable costs, which are volume-related (and are paid per quantity.)

In management accounting, _____ are defined as expenses that do not change in proportion to the activity of a business, within the relevant period or scale of production.

- a. Cost of quality
- b. Cost allocation
- c. Fixed costs
- d. Transaction cost

23. _____s are expenses that change in proportion to the activity of a business. In other words, _____ is the sum of marginal costs. It can also be considered normal costs.

a. Fixed costs
c. Cost overrun
b. Cost accounting
d. Variable Cost

Chapter 14. Inventory Systems for Independent Demand

1. An _____ is a manufacturing process in which parts (usually interchangeable parts) are added to a product in a sequential manner using optimally planned logistics to create a finished product much faster than with handcrafting-type methods. The _____ developed by Ford Motor Company between 1908 and 1915 made _____s famous in the following decade through the social ramifications of mass production, such as the affordability of the Ford Model T and the introduction of high wages for Ford workers. However, the various preconditions for the development at Ford stretched far back into the 19th century, from the gradual realization of the dream of interchangeability, to the concept of reinventing workflow and job descriptions using analytical methods.

   a. A Stake in the Outcome
   b. A4e
   c. AAAI
   d. Assembly line

2. _____ are goods that have completed the manufacturing process but have not yet been sold or distributed to the end user.

Manufacturing has three classes of inventory:

1. Raw material
2. Work in process
3. _____

A good purchased as a 'raw material' goes into the manufacture of a product. A good only partially completed during the manufacturing process is called 'work in process'. When the good is completed as to manufacturing but not yet sold or distributed to the end-user is called a 'finished good'.

   a. 28-hour day
   b. 1990 Clean Air Act
   c. Reorder point
   d. Finished goods

3. _____ or lean production, which is often known simply as 'Lean', is a production practice that considers the expenditure of resources for any goal other than the creation of value for the end customer to be wasteful, and thus a target for elimination. Working from the perspective of the customer who consumes a product or service, 'value' is defined as any action or process that a customer would be willing to pay for. Basically, lean is centered around creating more value with less work.

   a. Production line
   b. Six Sigma
   c. Theory of constraints
   d. Lean manufacturing

4. _____ is an advertisement in which a particular product specifically mentions a competitor by name for the express purpose of showing why the competitor is inferior to the product naming it.

This should not be confused with parody advertisements, where a fictional product is being advertised for the purpose of poking fun at the particular advertisement, nor should it be confused with the use of a coined brand name for the purpose of comparing the product without actually naming an actual competitor. ('Wikipedia tastes better and is less filling than the Encyclopedia Galactica.')

In the 1980s, during what has been referred to as the cola wars, soft-drink manufacturer Pepsi ran a series of advertisements where people, caught on hidden camera, in a blind taste test, chose Pepsi over rival Coca-Cola.

a. 33 Strategies of War
b. 1990 Clean Air Act
c. 28-hour day
d. Comparative advertising

5. In economics, business, retail, and accounting, a _____ is the value of money that has been used up to produce something, and hence is not available for use anymore. In economics, a _____ is an alternative that is given up as a result of a decision. In business, the _____ may be one of acquisition, in which case the amount of money expended to acquire it is counted as _____.
a. Cost allocation
b. Fixed costs
c. Cost overrun
d. Cost

6. _____ is the state of being which occurs when a person, object, or service is no longer wanted even though it may still be in good working order. _____ frequently occurs because a replacement has become available that is superior in one or more aspects. Videotapes making way for DVDs

Technical _____ may occur when a new product or technology supersedes the old, and it becomes preferred to utilize the new technology in place of the old.

a. A Stake in the Outcome
b. A4e
c. AAAI
d. Obsolescence

7. _____ is a costing model that identifies activities in an organization and assigns the cost of each activity resource to all products and services according to the actual consumption by each: it assigns more indirect costs (overhead) into direct costs.

In this way an organization can establish the true cost of its individual products and services for the purposes of identifying and eliminating those which are unprofitable and lowering the prices of those which are overpriced.

In a business organization, the ABC methodology assigns an organization's resource costs through activities to the products and services provided to its customers.

a. Activity-based costing
b. A Stake in the Outcome
c. Indirect costs
d. A4e

8. In economics, _____ is the desire to own something and the ability to pay for it. The term _____ signifies the ability or the willingness to buy a particular commodity at a given point of time.
a. 33 Strategies of War
b. 28-hour day
c. 1990 Clean Air Act
d. Demand

9. _____ is the process of estimation in unknown situations. Prediction is a similar, but more general term. Both can refer to estimation of time series, cross-sectional or longitudinal data.
a. 28-hour day
b. 1990 Clean Air Act
c. 33 Strategies of War
d. Forecasting

10. _____, a business term, is a measure of how products and services supplied by a company meet or surpass customer expectation. It is seen as a key performance indicator within business and is part of the four perspectives of a Balanced Scorecard.

Chapter 14. Inventory Systems for Independent Demand

In a competitive marketplace where businesses compete for customers, _____ is seen as a key differentiator and increasingly has become a key element of business strategy.

   a. Foreign ownership
   b. Horizontal integration
   c. Critical Success Factor
   d. Customer satisfaction

11. _____ is a business term used to define an inventory categorization technique often used in materials management.

_____ provides a mechanism for identifying items which will have a significant impact on overall inventory cost whilst also providing a mechanism for identifying different categories of stock that will require different management and controls

When carrying out an _____, inventory items are valued (item cost multiplied by quantity issued/consumed in period) with the results then ranked. The results are then grouped typically into three bands.

   a. A4e
   b. AAAI
   c. A Stake in the Outcome
   d. ABC analysis

12. _____ is the level of inventory that minimizes the total inventory holding costs and ordering costs. The framework used to determine this order quantity is also known as Wilson _____ Model. The model was developed by F. W. Harris in 1913.

   a. Anti-leadership
   b. Effective executive
   c. Event management
   d. Economic order quantity

13. In statistics, signal processing, and many other fields, a _____ is a sequence of data points, measured typically at successive times, spaced at (often uniform) time intervals. _____ analysis comprises methods that attempt to understand such _____, often either to understand the underlying context of the data points (Where did they come from? What generated them?), or to make forecasts (predictions.) _____ forecasting is the use of a model to forecast future events based on known past events: to forecast future data points before they are measured.

   a. Histogram
   b. Time series
   c. Standard deviation
   d. Moving average

14. In statistics, signal processing, and many other fields, a time series is a sequence of data points, measured typically at successive times, spaced at (often uniform) time intervals. _____ comprises methods that attempt to understand such time series, often either to understand the underlying context of the data points (Where did they come from? What generated them?), or to make forecasts (predictions.) Time series forecasting is the use of a model to forecast future events based on known past events: to forecast future data points before they are measured.

   a. Correlation
   b. Time series analysis
   c. Failure rate
   d. Moving average

15. _____ is a term used by inventory specialists to describe a level of extra stock that is maintained below the cycle stock to buffer against stockouts. _____ exists to counter uncertainties in supply and demand. _____ is defined as extra units of inventory carried as protection against possible stockouts .(shortfall in raw material or packaging.)

Chapter 14. Inventory Systems for Independent Demand

a. Knowledge worker
c. Safety stock
b. Process automation
d. Product life cycle

16. _____ is the process of understanding, anticipating and influencing consumer behavior in order to maximize revenue or profits from a fixed, perishable resource This process was first discovered by Dr. Matt H. Keller. The challenge is to sell the right resources to the right customer at the right time for the right price.

a. Gap analysis
c. Business model design
b. Yield management
d. Business networking

17. The _____ states that, for many events, roughly 80% of the effects come from 20% of the causes. Business management thinker Joseph M. Juran suggested the principle and named it after Italian economist Vilfredo Pareto, who observed that 80% of the land in Italy was owned by 20% of the population. It is a common rule of thumb in business; e.g., '80% of your sales come from 20% of your clients.' Mathematically, where something is shared among a sufficiently large set of participants, there will always be a number k between 50 and 100 such that k% is taken by% of the participants.

a. Greenfield agreement
c. Bylaw
b. Board of directors
d. Pareto Principle

18. Procter is a surname, and may also refer to:

- Bryan Waller Procter (pseud. Barry Cornwall), English poet
- Goodwin Procter, American law firm
- _____, consumer products multinational

a. Master and Servant Acts
c. Strict liability
b. Downstream
d. Procter ' Gamble

19. _____ is, in very basic words, a position a firm occupies against its competitors.

According to Michael Porter, the three methods for creating a sustainable _____ are through:

1. Cost leadership

2. Differentiation

3. Focus (economics)

a. 28-hour day
c. 1990 Clean Air Act
b. Theory Z
d. Competitive advantage

20. _____, in microeconomics, are the cost advantages that a business obtains due to expansion. They are factors that cause a producer's average cost per unit to fall as scale is increased. _____ is a long run concept and refers to reductions in unit cost as the size of a facility, or scale, increases.

a. A4e
c. Economies of scope
b. A Stake in the Outcome
d. Economies of scale

21. _____ is a company-wide computer software system used to manage and coordinate all the resources, information, and functions of a business from shared data stores.

An _____ system has a service-oriented architecture with modular hardware and software units and 'services' that communicate on a local area network. The modular design allows a business to add or reconfigure modules (perhaps from different vendors) while preserving data integrity in one shared database that may be centralized or distributed.

a. A Stake in the Outcome
b. AAAI
c. A4e
d. Enterprise resource planning

Chapter 15. Inventory Systems for Dependent Demand

1. _____, also known as Merck Sharp ' Dohme or MSD outside the USA and Canada, is one of the largest pharmaceutical companies in the world. The headquarters of the company is located in Whitehouse Station, New Jersey, an unincorporated area in Readington Township.

   a. Goodrich Corporation   b. National Whistleblower Center
   c. Merck ' Co., Inc.   d. Quest Diagnostics

2. _____ is a company-wide computer software system used to manage and coordinate all the resources, information, and functions of a business from shared data stores.

An _____ system has a service-oriented architecture with modular hardware and software units and 'services' that communicate on a local area network. The modular design allows a business to add or reconfigure modules (perhaps from different vendors) while preserving data integrity in one shared database that may be centralized or distributed.

   a. A Stake in the Outcome   b. AAAI
   c. Enterprise resource planning   d. A4e

3. _____ is, in very basic words, a position a firm occupies against its competitors.

According to Michael Porter, the three methods for creating a sustainable _____ are through:

1. Cost leadership

2. Differentiation

3. Focus (economics)

   a. Competitive advantage   b. 1990 Clean Air Act
   c. 28-hour day   d. Theory Z

4. _____, a business term, is a measure of how products and services supplied by a company meet or surpass customer expectation. It is seen as a key performance indicator within business and is part of the four perspectives of a Balanced Scorecard.

In a competitive marketplace where businesses compete for customers, _____ is seen as a key differentiator and increasingly has become a key element of business strategy.

   a. Foreign ownership   b. Horizontal integration
   c. Critical Success Factor   d. Customer satisfaction

5. Manufacturing Resource Planning (_____) is defined by APICS as a method for the effective planning of all resources of a manufacturing company. Ideally, it addresses operational planning in units, financial planning in dollars, and has a simulation capability to answer 'what-if' questions and extension of closed-loop MRP. Manufacturing Resource Planning (or MRP2) - Around 1980, over-frequent changes in sales forecasts, entailing continual readjustments in production, as well as the unsuitability of the parameters fixed by the system, led MRP (Material Requirement Planning) to evolve into a new concept : Manufacturing Resource Planning (e.g. MRP 2)

Chapter 15. Inventory Systems for Dependent Demand 113

This is not exclusively a software function, but a marriage of people skills, dedication to data base accuracy, and computer resources.

a. Homeworkers
b. MRP II
c. Jidoka
d. Manufacturing resource planning

6. A _____ is a plan for production, staffing, inventory, etc. It is usually linked to manufacturing where the plan indicates when and how much of each product will be demanded. This plan quantifies significant processes, parts, and other resources in order to optimize production, to identify bottlenecks, and to anticipate needs and completed goods.
a. Value engineering
b. Piecework
c. Remanufacturing
d. Master production schedule

7. _____ is a list of the raw materials, sub-assemblies, intermediate assemblies, sub-components, components, parts and the quantities of each needed to manufacture an end item (final product).
a. Bill of materials
b. Methods-time measurement
c. Scientific management
d. Piece rate

8. In economics, _____ is the desire to own something and the ability to pay for it. The term _____ signifies the ability or the willingness to buy a particular commodity at a given point of time.
a. 1990 Clean Air Act
b. 33 Strategies of War
c. 28-hour day
d. Demand

9. _____ is the process of estimation in unknown situations. Prediction is a similar, but more general term. Both can refer to estimation of time series, cross-sectional or longitudinal data.
a. 1990 Clean Air Act
b. 28-hour day
c. 33 Strategies of War
d. Forecasting

10. _____ generally refers to a list of all planned expenses and revenues. It is a plan for saving and spending. A _____ is an important concept in microeconomics, which uses a _____ line to illustrate the trade-offs between two or more goods.
a. 28-hour day
b. 33 Strategies of War
c. Budget
d. 1990 Clean Air Act

11. _____ is an integrated business management process through which the executive/leadership team continually achieves focus, alignment and synchronization among all the functions of the organization. The monthly S'OP plan includes an updated sales plan, production plan, inventory plan, customer lead time (backlog) plan, new product development plan, strategic initiative plan and resulting financial plan. Done well, the S'OP process also enables effective supply chain management.
a. 33 Strategies of War
b. 1990 Clean Air Act
c. Sales and operations planning
d. 28-hour day

12. _____ is a business term used to define an inventory categorization technique often used in materials management.

Chapter 15. Inventory Systems for Dependent Demand

_____ provides a mechanism for identifying items which will have a significant impact on overall inventory cost whilst also providing a mechanism for identifying different categories of stock that will require different management and controls

When carrying out an _____, inventory items are valued (item cost multiplied by quantity issued/consumed in period) with the results then ranked. The results are then grouped typically into three bands.

- a. A4e
- b. ABC analysis
- c. A Stake in the Outcome
- d. AAAI

13. _____ is the level of inventory that minimizes the total inventory holding costs and ordering costs. The framework used to determine this order quantity is also known as Wilson _____ Model. The model was developed by F. W. Harris in 1913.
- a. Economic order quantity
- b. Effective executive
- c. Event management
- d. Anti-leadership

14. _____ is an advertisement in which a particular product specifically mentions a competitor by name for the express purpose of showing why the competitor is inferior to the product naming it.

This should not be confused with parody advertisements, where a fictional product is being advertised for the purpose of poking fun at the particular advertisement, nor should it be confused with the use of a coined brand name for the purpose of comparing the product without actually naming an actual competitor. ('Wikipedia tastes better and is less filling than the Encyclopedia Galactica.')

In the 1980s, during what has been referred to as the cola wars, soft-drink manufacturer Pepsi ran a series of advertisements where people, caught on hidden camera, in a blind taste test, chose Pepsi over rival Coca-Cola.

- a. 1990 Clean Air Act
- b. Comparative advertising
- c. 28-hour day
- d. 33 Strategies of War

Chapter 16. Waiting Line Management

1. _____, a business term, is a measure of how products and services supplied by a company meet or surpass customer expectation. It is seen as a key performance indicator within business and is part of the four perspectives of a Balanced Scorecard.

In a competitive marketplace where businesses compete for customers, _____ is seen as a key differentiator and increasingly has become a key element of business strategy.

a. Critical Success Factor
b. Horizontal integration
c. Customer satisfaction
d. Foreign ownership

2. _____ is an advertisement in which a particular product specifically mentions a competitor by name for the express purpose of showing why the competitor is inferior to the product naming it.

This should not be confused with parody advertisements, where a fictional product is being advertised for the purpose of poking fun at the particular advertisement, nor should it be confused with the use of a coined brand name for the purpose of comparing the product without actually naming an actual competitor. ('Wikipedia tastes better and is less filling than the Encyclopedia Galactica.')

In the 1980s, during what has been referred to as the cola wars, soft-drink manufacturer Pepsi ran a series of advertisements where people, caught on hidden camera, in a blind taste test, chose Pepsi over rival Coca-Cola.

a. 33 Strategies of War
b. 1990 Clean Air Act
c. 28-hour day
d. Comparative advertising

3. _____ is the provision of service to customers before, during and after a purchase.

According to Turban et al. (2002), '_____ is a series of activities designed to enhance the level of customer satisfaction - that is, the feeling that a product or service has met the customer expectation.'

Its importance varies by product, industry and customer; defective or broken merchandise can be exchanged, often only with a receipt and within a specified time frame.

a. 28-hour day
b. Service rate
c. Customer service
d. 1990 Clean Air Act

4. A _____ or business method is a collection of related, structured activities or tasks that produce a specific service or product (serve a particular goal) for a particular customer or customers. It often can be visualized with a flowchart as a sequence of activities.

Chapter 16. Waiting Line Management

There are three types of _____es:

1. Management processes, the processes that govern the operation of a system. Typical management processes include 'Corporate Governance' and 'Strategic Management'.
2. Operational processes, processes that constitute the core business and create the primary value stream. Typical operational processes are Purchasing, Manufacturing, Marketing, and Sales.
3. Supporting processes, which support the core processes. Examples include Accounting, Recruitment, Technical support.

A _____ begins with a customer's need and ends with a customer's need fulfillment. Process oriented organizations break down the barriers of structural departments and try to avoid functional silos.

- a. Business process
- b. 1990 Clean Air Act
- c. 33 Strategies of War
- d. 28-hour day

5. In organizational development (OD), _____ is the application of Socio-Technical Systems principles and techniques to the humanization of work.

The aims of _____ to improved job satisfaction, to improved through-put, to improved quality and to reduced employee problems, e.g., grievances, absenteeism.

Under scientific management people would be directed by reason and the problems of industrial unrest would be appropriately (i.e., scientifically) addressed.

- a. Management process
- b. Graduate recruitment
- c. Work design
- d. Path-goal theory

6. _____ refers to training in different ways to improve overall performance. It takes advantage of the particular effectiveness of each training method, while at the same time attempting to neglect the shortcomings of that method by combining it with other methods that address its weaknesses.

Cross training is employee-employer field means, training employees to do one another's work.

- a. 33 Strategies of War
- b. 28-hour day
- c. 1990 Clean Air Act
- d. Cross-training

7. _____ consists of the sale of goods or merchandise from a fixed location, such as a department store, boutique or kiosk in small or individual lots for direct consumption by the purchaser. _____ may include subordinated services, such as delivery. Purchasers may be individuals or businesses.
- a. Retailing
- b. Planogram
- c. 28-hour day
- d. 1990 Clean Air Act

8. _____ is, in very basic words, a position a firm occupies against its competitors.

Chapter 16. Waiting Line Management

According to Michael Porter, the three methods for creating a sustainable _____ are through:

1. Cost leadership

2. Differentiation

3. Focus (economics)

    a. 28-hour day   b. Competitive advantage
    c. Theory Z   d. 1990 Clean Air Act

9. An _____ is a manufacturing process in which parts (usually interchangeable parts) are added to a product in a sequential manner using optimally planned logistics to create a finished product much faster than with handcrafting-type methods. The _____ developed by Ford Motor Company between 1908 and 1915 made _____s famous in the following decade through the social ramifications of mass production, such as the affordability of the Ford Model T and the introduction of high wages for Ford workers. However, the various preconditions for the development at Ford stretched far back into the 19th century, from the gradual realization of the dream of interchangeability, to the concept of reinventing workflow and job descriptions using analytical methods.

    a. A Stake in the Outcome   b. AAAI
    c. Assembly line   d. A4e

10. In business, _____ is a performance metric used to measure the customer service in a supply organization. One example of a _____ measures the number of units filled as a percentage of the total ordered and is known as fill rate. If customer orders total 1000 units, and you can only meet 900 units of that order, your fill rate is 90%.

- In statistics, notably in queuing theory, _____ denotes the rate at which customers are being served in a system. It is the reciprocal of the service time. For example, a supermarket cash desk with an average service time of 30 seconds per customer would have an average _____ of 2 per minute. In statistics the greek letter >µ is used for the _____.

    a. Customer service   b. 28-hour day
    c. Service rate   d. 1990 Clean Air Act

11. In queueing theory, _____ is the proportion of the system's resources which is used by the traffic which arrives at it. It should be strictly less than one for the system to function well. It is usually represented by the symbol ρ.

    a. Utilization   b. AAAI
    c. A Stake in the Outcome   d. A4e

Chapter 17. Scheduling

1. _____ is the level of inventory that minimizes the total inventory holding costs and ordering costs. The framework used to determine this order quantity is also known as Wilson _____ Model. The model was developed by F. W. Harris in 1913.
   a. Event management
   b. Effective executive
   c. Economic order quantity
   d. Anti-leadership

2. _____ are typically small manufacturing operations that handle specialized manufacturing processes such as small customer orders or small batch jobs. _____ typically move on to different jobs (possibly with different customers) when each job is completed. By nature of this type of manufacturing operation, _____ are usually specialized in skill and processes.
   a. 28-hour day
   b. 33 Strategies of War
   c. 1990 Clean Air Act
   d. Job shops

3. A _____ is a plan for production, staffing, inventory, etc. It is usually linked to manufacturing where the plan indicates when and how much of each product will be demanded. This plan quantifies significant processes, parts, and other resources in order to optimize production, to identify bottlenecks, and to anticipate needs and completed goods.
   a. Piecework
   b. Value engineering
   c. Remanufacturing
   d. Master production schedule

4. _____ is an advertisement in which a particular product specifically mentions a competitor by name for the express purpose of showing why the competitor is inferior to the product naming it.

This should not be confused with parody advertisements, where a fictional product is being advertised for the purpose of poking fun at the particular advertisement, nor should it be confused with the use of a coined brand name for the purpose of comparing the product without actually naming an actual competitor. ('Wikipedia tastes better and is less filling than the Encyclopedia Galactica.')

In the 1980s, during what has been referred to as the cola wars, soft-drink manufacturer Pepsi ran a series of advertisements where people, caught on hidden camera, in a blind taste test, chose Pepsi over rival Coca-Cola.

   a. 33 Strategies of War
   b. Comparative advertising
   c. 1990 Clean Air Act
   d. 28-hour day

5. _____ is one of the managerial functions like planning, organizing, staffing and directing. It is an important function because it helps to check the errors and to take the corrective action so that deviation from standards are minimized and stated goals of the organization are achieved in desired manner. According to modern concepts, _____ is a foreseeing action whereas earlier concept of _____ was used only when errors were detected. _____ in management means setting standards, measuring actual performance and taking corrective action.
   a. Control
   b. Schedule of reinforcement
   c. Turnover
   d. Decision tree pruning

6. A _____ or labor union is an organization of workers who have banded together to achieve common goals in key areas and working conditions. The _____, through its leadership, bargains with the employer on behalf of union members (rank and file members) and negotiates labor contracts (Collective bargaining) with employers. This may include the negotiation of wages, work rules, complaint procedures, rules governing hiring, firing and promotion of workers, benefits, workplace safety and policies.

Chapter 17. Scheduling

a. Trade union
b. Labour law
c. Working time
d. Company union

7. _____ is a concept related to lean and just-in-time (JIT) production. The Japanese word _____ is a common term meaning 'signboard' or 'billboard'. According to Taiichi Ohno, the man credited with developing JIT, _____ is a means through which JIT is achieved.
a. Trademark
b. Succession planning
c. Risk management
d. Kanban

8. In economics, _____s are key economic variables that economists used to predict a new phase of the business cycle. A _____ is one that changes before the economy does; a lagging indicator is one that changes after the economy has changed. Examples of _____s include stock prices, which often improve or worsen before a similar change in the economy.
a. Deflation
b. Leading indicator
c. Human capital
d. Perfect competition

9. _____ is an overall management philosophy introduced by Dr. Eliyahu M. Goldratt in his 1984 book titled The Goal, that is geared to help organizations continually achieve their goal. The title comes from the contention that any manageable system is limited in achieving more of its goal by a very small number of constraints, and that there is always at least one constraint. The _____ process seeks to identify the constraint and restructure the rest of the organization around it, through the use of the Five Focusing Steps.
a. Production line
b. Takt time
c. Six Sigma
d. Theory of constraints

10. An _____ is a manufacturing process in which parts (usually interchangeable parts) are added to a product in a sequential manner using optimally planned logistics to create a finished product much faster than with handcrafting-type methods. The _____ developed by Ford Motor Company between 1908 and 1915 made _____s famous in the following decade through the social ramifications of mass production, such as the affordability of the Ford Model T and the introduction of high wages for Ford workers. However, the various preconditions for the development at Ford stretched far back into the 19th century, from the gradual realization of the dream of interchangeability, to the concept of reinventing workflow and job descriptions using analytical methods.
a. AAAI
b. Assembly line
c. A4e
d. A Stake in the Outcome

11. A _____ is a type of bar chart that illustrates a project schedule. _____s illustrate the start and finish dates of the terminal elements and summary elements of a project. Terminal elements and summary elements comprise the work breakdown structure of the project.
a. 33 Strategies of War
b. Gantt chart
c. 1990 Clean Air Act
d. 28-hour day

12. _____ is the process of estimation in unknown situations. Prediction is a similar, but more general term. Both can refer to estimation of time series, cross-sectional or longitudinal data.
a. 1990 Clean Air Act
b. 28-hour day
c. 33 Strategies of War
d. Forecasting

Chapter 17. Scheduling

13. In statistics, signal processing, and many other fields, a _____ is a sequence of data points, measured typically at successive times, spaced at (often uniform) time intervals. _____ analysis comprises methods that attempt to understand such _____, often either to understand the underlying context of the data points (Where did they come from? What generated them?), or to make forecasts (predictions.) _____ forecasting is the use of a model to forecast future events based on known past events: to forecast future data points before they are measured.
   - a. Moving average
   - b. Standard deviation
   - c. Histogram
   - d. Time series

14. In statistics, signal processing, and many other fields, a time series is a sequence of data points, measured typically at successive times, spaced at (often uniform) time intervals. _____ comprises methods that attempt to understand such time series, often either to understand the underlying context of the data points (Where did they come from? What generated them?), or to make forecasts (predictions.) Time series forecasting is the use of a model to forecast future events based on known past events: to forecast future data points before they are measured.
   - a. Failure rate
   - b. Moving average
   - c. Correlation
   - d. Time series analysis

15. In economics, _____ is the desire to own something and the ability to pay for it. The term _____ signifies the ability or the willingness to buy a particular commodity at a given point of time.
   - a. 28-hour day
   - b. 1990 Clean Air Act
   - c. 33 Strategies of War
   - d. Demand

16. Manufacturing Resource Planning (_____) is defined by APICS as a method for the effective planning of all resources of a manufacturing company. Ideally, it addresses operational planning in units, financial planning in dollars, and has a simulation capability to answer 'what-if' questions and extension of closed-loop MRP. Manufacturing Resource Planning (or MRP2) - Around 1980, over-frequent changes in sales forecasts, entailing continual readjustments in production, as well as the unsuitability of the parameters fixed by the system, led MRP (Material Requirement Planning) to evolve into a new concept : Manufacturing Resource Planning (e.g. MRP 2)

This is not exclusively a software function, but a marriage of people skills, dedication to data base accuracy, and computer resources.
   - a. Homeworkers
   - b. Manufacturing resource planning
   - c. Jidoka
   - d. MRP II

17. The _____ of 1938 (_____, ch. 676, 52 Stat. 1060, June 25, 1938, 29 U.S.C. ch.8), also called the Wages and Hours Bill, is United States federal law that applies to employees engaged in interstate commerce or employed by an enterprise engaged in commerce or in the production of goods for commerce, unless the employer can claim an exemption from coverage. The _____ established a national minimum wage, guaranteed time and a half for overtime in certain jobs, and prohibited most employment of minors in 'oppressive child labor,' a term defined in the statute.
   - a. Fair Labor Standards Act
   - b. Board of directors
   - c. Family and Medical Leave Act of 1993
   - d. Joint venture

18. _____ are conventions, treaties and recommendations designed to eliminate unjust and inhumane labour practices. The primary inernational agency charged with developing such standards is the International Labour Organization (ILO.) Established in 1919, the ILO advocates international standards as essential for the eradication of labour conditions involving 'injustice, hardship and privation'.

a. Anaconda Copper
b. Airbus Industrie
c. International labour standards
d. Airbus SAS

19. _____ is the value on a given date of a future payment or series of future payments, discounted to reflect the time value of money and other factors such as investment risk. _____ calculations are widely used in business and economics to provide a means to compare cash flows at different times on a meaningful 'like to like' basis.

If offered a choice between $100 today or $100 in one year, everyone will choose $100 today.

a. Net present value
b. Present value
c. 1990 Clean Air Act
d. Discounted cash flow

20. In probability theory and statistics, the _____ or Gaussian distribution is a continuous probability distribution that describes data that clusters around a mean or average. The graph of the associated probability density function is bell-shaped, with a peak at the mean, and is known as the Gaussian function or bell curve.

The _____ can be used to describe, at least approximately, any variable that tends to cluster around the mean.

a. Histogram
b. Heteroskedastic
c. Generalized normal distribution
d. Normal distribution

21. _____ is one of the four elements of marketing mix. An organization or set of organizations (go-betweens) involved in the process of making a product or service available for use or consumption by a consumer or business user.

The other three parts of the marketing mix are product, pricing, and promotion.

a. Missing completely at random
b. Matching theory
c. Distribution
d. Job creation programs

Chapter 1

1. d	2. c	3. d	4. c	5. d	6. d	7. d	8. d	9. d	10. d
11. c	12. d	13. c	14. b	15. c	16. b	17. d	18. b	19. a	20. d
21. b	22. d	23. b	24. d	25. d	26. b	27. c	28. b	29. a	30. d
31. d	32. d								

Chapter 2

1. d	2. d	3. c	4. d	5. d	6. d	7. d	8. d	9. b	10. d
11. d	12. c	13. d	14. d	15. a	16. d	17. d	18. d	19. d	20. d
21. d	22. c	23. b	24. d	25. d	26. d	27. c	28. d	29. a	30. b
31. d	32. d	33. d	34. b	35. b	36. c	37. a	38. b	39. d	40. c
41. a	42. c	43. b	44. b	45. c	46. b	47. d	48. c	49. d	50. c
51. d	52. d	53. d	54. b	55. b	56. c	57. d	58. d	59. c	60. d

Chapter 3

1. c	2. d	3. d	4. c	5. d	6. d	7. d	8. c	9. b	10. b
11. d	12. d	13. c	14. a	15. b	16. d	17. c	18. c	19. c	20. d
21. b	22. c	23. d	24. c	25. a	26. c	27. d	28. d	29. c	30. c
31. b	32. b	33. b	34. d	35. d	36. d	37. d	38. d	39. c	40. d
41. a	42. d	43. d	44. d	45. d	46. a	47. d			

Chapter 4

1. d	2. d	3. d	4. d	5. d	6. d	7. d	8. d	9. a	10. b
11. d	12. a	13. b	14. a	15. a	16. b	17. d	18. d	19. b	20. d
21. d	22. b	23. b	24. b	25. a	26. b	27. d	28. c	29. d	30. d
31. c	32. c	33. d	34. a	35. b	36. b	37. d	38. c	39. b	40. c
41. b									

Chapter 5

| 1. d | 2. b | 3. a | 4. d | 5. d | 6. a | 7. d | 8. d | 9. d | 10. d |
| 11. c | 12. c | 13. b | 14. c | 15. d | | | | | |

Chapter 6

1. c	2. d	3. d	4. b	5. d	6. a	7. d	8. d	9. b	10. d
11. b	12. d	13. a	14. a	15. d	16. c	17. b	18. a	19. d	20. d
21. b	22. c	23. c	24. d	25. c	26. b	27. a	28. b	29. d	30. d
31. d	32. c								

Chapter 7

1. d	2. d	3. b	4. d	5. c	6. d	7. d	8. c	9. d	10. c
11. b	12. c	13. d	14. d	15. b	16. d	17. d	18. d	19. b	20. d
21. c	22. b	23. d	24. d						

ANSWER KEY

Chapter 8
1. c   2. d   3. a   4. a   5. b   6. c   7. d   8. c   9. b   10. b
11. d 12. b 13. a 14. d 15. d 16. c 17. b 18. d 19. b 20. d
21. c 22. d 23. a 24. d 25. a 26. a 27. a 28. d 29. d 30. c
31. d 32. a 33. d 34. d 35. d 36. b 37. d

Chapter 9
1. d   2. b   3. d   4. c   5. a   6. d   7. a   8. d   9. d   10. d
11. d 12. d 13. a 14. d 15. d 16. a 17. d 18. b 19. a 20. d
21. d 22. b 23. c 24. a 25. d 26. d 27. c 28. d 29. d 30. b
31. c 32. b 33. d 34. d 35. d 36. c 37. d 38. b 39. c 40. a
41. d 42. b 43. a 44. d 45. a 46. b 47. d 48. a 49. b 50. a
51. c 52. a 53. d 54. c 55. d 56. c

Chapter 10
1. c   2. d   3. b   4. d   5. d   6. d   7. d   8. d   9. a   10. d
11. c 12. d 13. d 14. d 15. d 16. c 17. b 18. d 19. d 20. d
21. d 22. d 23. b 24. c 25. d 26. c 27. a 28. d 29. d 30. d

Chapter 11
1. c   2. b   3. a   4. a   5. d   6. a   7. d   8. d   9. d   10. d
11. b 12. d 13. a 14. d 15. d 16. a 17. d 18. b 19. b 20. c
21. d 22. d 23. d 24. b 25. d 26. b 27. d 28. d

Chapter 12
1. d   2. d   3. b   4. d   5. d   6. d   7. d   8. a   9. c   10. a
11. b 12. a 13. b 14. a 15. c 16. d 17. d 18. a 19. c 20. b
21. d 22. d 23. c 24. d 25. d 26. d 27. d 28. d 29. d 30. c
31. a 32. d 33. b

Chapter 13
1. d   2. c   3. b   4. c   5. d   6. c   7. d   8. c   9. d   10. b
11. a 12. c 13. d 14. a 15. d 16. d 17. d 18. b 19. c 20. c
21. c 22. c 23. d

Chapter 14
1. d   2. d   3. d   4. d   5. d   6. d   7. a   8. d   9. d   10. d
11. d 12. d 13. b 14. b 15. c 16. b 17. d 18. d 19. d 20. d
21. d

Chapter 15
1. c   2. c   3. a   4. d   5. b   6. d   7. a   8. d   9. d   10. c
11. c 12. b 13. a 14. b

Chapter 16
1. c 2. d 3. c 4. a 5. c 6. d 7. a 8. b 9. c 10. c
11. a

Chapter 17
1. c 2. d 3. d 4. b 5. a 6. a 7. d 8. b 9. d 10. b
11. b 12. d 13. d 14. d 15. d 16. d 17. a 18. c 19. b 20. d
21. c

www.ingramcontent.com/pod-product-compliance
Lightning Source LLC
Chambersburg PA
CBHW082047230426
43670CB00016B/2809